TURBO MNEMONICS FOR THE BOARDS:

OVER 400 MEMORY AIDS TO THE MOST COMMONLY ASKED MATERIAL ON THE <u>USMLE CLINICAL STEPS &</u> <u>INTERNAL MEDICINE BOARDS</u>

BRADLEY D. MITTMAN, M.D.

THIRD EDITION

FRONTRUNNERS PUBLISHING/ FBRI
23511 Aliso Creek Rd.
Aliso Viejo, CA 92656

PREFACE

Hailed as "The Ultimate Review for Boards & Other exams, this book was designed to help you retain better and recall faster. Whether your goal is to nail your **USMLE** clinical steps 2 & 3 or your **MEDICINE BOARDS**, or you simply want to be the star on rounds & attending pimp sessions, we guarantee Turbo Mnemonics will *markedly* improve your study efficiency, win you a lot more points, improve your performance on rotations and teaching rounds, and help you reach that goal a whole lot *faster and* with a lot less headaches!

This book was created in order to make your study life *and* your medicine career easier. With **over 400 anagrams and other mnemonics**, tips, tricks, and shortcuts, this book **LITERALLY spells out** what you'll *have* to know for the medicine components of your **USMLE** steps 2 & 3, and the   **MEDICINE BOARDS**. Indeed, if you're prepping *now* for the USMLE, you'll be *way ahead* of the game when it comes time to take your medicine boards.

As you **browse this book**, you'll find over 400 priceless memory aids on all your favorite subjects organized **alphabetically by the disease** or condition. In addition, you'll *definitely* want take advantage of the **APPENDIX section**, which features a **summary** of all the memory aids found in the book with their page numbers to help you **quickly locate** your favorite mnemonics or just the information you need! Of course you may simply choose to take advantage of the well-designed and thorough Index section as a final means of look-up.

Most of us would agree that intelligence & performance don't *necessarily* jive when it comes to standardized exams. Sure, brains matter. Of course, study time matters. But the most important element, of course, has always been WHAT you study, that is, what **mental tools** you take into the exam with you. Turbo Mnemonics is your tool-kit. Even if you *only* choose 20 favorite mnemonics / pages from the 400 here (!) to learn, you can easily increase your board scores by 20 points alone. For this book in particular, the ink coverage and therefore your time spent studying, is minimal. It's designed for maximal study efficiency. And don't forget to take advantage of the Appendix section to help you *quickly locate* your favorite mnemonics or just the information you need!

Most of us remember what a lifesaver mnemonics were during our basic sciences, particularly when it came time for exams and tensions were running high. Memory aids saved us tons of **time** and always improved **performance**. Astonishingly, there are few such resources available in *clinical* medicine, particularly when it comes to board preparation, certainly not on this magnitude. Clinical mnemonics aren't *just* important because they help you remember better and recall quicker. They serve two <u>other</u> very important roles. *First*, they function as **templates** to help you efficiently sort thru the nonsense and get o those key features the boards always want you to know for any given disease. *Secondly*, clinical mnemonics provide a sound **framework** on which to **build** your ever-growing medical knowledge base. As you acquire new info, you'll know exactly where to hang it in on your framework and you'll see exactly how it fits into the "big picture".

Like to find out more about Frontrunners board review courses or other product offerings? Just visit us at www.frontrunners.info and click on either the "**Product Vault**" or "**Course Info**" tabs. There you'll not only be able to view and even hear samples of all our products, but you can quickly and easily place your orders from the Product Vault page. You can also flip to very last page of <u>this</u> book to view ordering information on: 1) **Frontrunners 2005-2006 Internal Medicine Q&A REVIEW For The Boards**, featuring > 1300 realistically-designed Q&A to prepare you; and 2) **Frontrunners 2005-2006 Audio/Visual CDs For The Boards**. Enjoy these resources; learn them cold; and excel.

Here's to you achieving <u>all</u> your goals in medicine.   We'll see you at the top!

Bradley D. Mittman, MD
Bradley D. Mittman, MD
FRONTRUNNERS BOARD REVIEW, INC.

• NOTICE •

Dedication

To my Mom,
who hasn't stopped calling since the day I went away to college. Through your many examples, I've learned the meaning of sacrifice, perseverance & excellence. Thank you, especially, for all the opportunities you gave me early on in both sports & academics.

I love you for all your support.

TABLE OF CONTENTS:

Quick Order Form

A-a (ALVEOLAR-ARTERIAL) GRADIENT: DIFFERENTIAL: VSD

V /Q mismatch
1. PE
2. Airway obstruction (asthma, COPD)
3. Interstitial lung disease
4. Alveolar disease

S hunt
1. Intracardiac (e.g. **VSD !**)
2. Intrapulmonary shunt (e.g. ARDS or intrapulmonary AVM) and intraalveolar filling (pus=pneumonia; water=CHF; protein (AP); blood)
3. Alveolar collapse (atelectasis)

D iffusion defect, e.g.
1. IPF
2. Emphysema

ALLERGIC BRONCHOPULMONARY ASPERGILLOSIS (ABPA): ABPA PIES

A sthma, severe, refractory hypersensitivity to aspergillus found in the lung.

B rown mucus plugs; Bronchiectasis (central)

P ulmonary infiltrates—recurrent, migratory

A spergillus hypersensitivity (ie hypersensitivity to Aspergillus colonizing the tracheobronchial airways (not the distal airways) which may mimic asthma and chronic bronchitis.

P recipitating antibodies to A. fumigatus in the blood (most specific test for ABPA, may be masked by steroid therapy)

I mmediate type; wheel & flare; type I; IgE;) and type III (Antigen/Antibody complex) hypersensitivity reactions can be demonstrated to Aspergillus; Impaction (mucoid); Immunoglobulins: total Ig G and Ig E are ↑

E class immunoglobulins (IgE) ↑ (≥ 1000 IU/dL); Eos (peripheral) ↑ (> 8%); may also be masked by steroid therapy

S teroids (there is NO role for antifungal therapy in ABPA)

ABDOMINAL ANGINA (INTESTINAL ANGINA):   CLAMPS

C hronic mesenteric insufficiency (aka)

L asts several hours

A bdominal angiogram usually demonstrates complete or near complete occlusion of at least two of the three major splanchnic arteries, usually the celiac and superior mesenteric arteries.

M idabdominal pain that occurs 15-30 minutes after eating due to insufficient postprandial mucosal blood flow. Mechanisms that have been proposed to explain the postprandial timing of the intestinal angina include: 1) mismatch between splanchnic blood flow and intestinal metabolic demand; and 2) small intestinal hypoperfusion from the shunting of blood to the stomach.

P VD or CAD in approximately half of these patients

S imilar to angina pectoris, the pain occurs under conditions of increased demand for splanchnic blood flow.

ACE INHIBITOR—CONTRAINDICATIONS: ACE wRAP

W

R enal artery stenosis

A llergy (h/o ACEI—associated or other angioedema); Anuria

P regnancy, Preexisting hyperkalemia

ACHALASIA: BEAST, MD

B ird's beak sign on UGI = dilated esophagus with tapered lower end, caused by persistently contracted Lower Esophageal Sphinctor (LES)

E ndoscopic evaluation is a must in making the diagnosis, as malignancies of the EG junction can mimic primary achalasia clinically, radiographically, and manometrically (so-called "pseudoachalasia")

A spiration often seen at night

S quamous cell esophageal carcinoma can complicate

T reatment options: 1) Botulin toxin injection (Botox®); 2) bougienage; 3) pneumatic dilatation; 4) surgical myotomy; and 5) medical therapy with nitrates or calcium channel blockers.

M anometry: 3 characteristic features:

    1. HIGH resting LES pressure

    2. Incomplete LES relaxation

    3. Aperistalsis is seen in the smooth muscle portion of the body of the esophagus. Tertiary contractions may be seen replacing peristaltic activity at all levels.

D ysphagia is to both solids and liquids; Definition of Achalasia (Greek): "does not relax"

CAUSES OF ACQUIRED AT III (ANTITHROMBIN III) DEFICIENCY: NO PHD

N   ephrotic syndrome

O   CPs

T   hrombosis, massive

P   regnancy

H   epatic disease, heparin therapy

D   IC

ACQUIRED DISORDERS ASSOCIATED WITH HYPERHOMOCYSTINEMIA:

"HYPER C.H.A.D."

C RF; CAD & CVA

H ypothyroidism

A nemia, pernicious; Age

D ietary deficiencies in folate, B6, or B12; DVT; Drugs (methotrexate, phenytoin, carbamazepine)

ACROMEGALY—*Clinical Presentation* (2° to GH/IGF-1 excess):   **PM SNACK**

P rolactinemia (in up to half the cases), causing amenorrhea / ↓libido / galactorrhea; Pituitary mass effect: Headaches, visual impairment, hypopituitarism (manifested as hypogonadism/ hypothyroidism/ hypoadrenalism)

M yopathy (proximal)

S weating ↑, oily Skin; Skin tags
Sleep apnea

N erve entrapment syndromes, esp carpal tunnel syndrome

A cromegalic features
Acroparesthesias; Acral enlargement; Acanthosis Nigricans (other causes of A.N. are obesity; DM; gastric ca)

C arbohydrate intolerance / diabetes mellitus (*pm snack!*) in 20%
↓ Heat tolerance
Cardiovascular complications: Cardiomyopathy; HTN

K inds of carcinomas predisposed to: esophagus, stomach, colon, melanoma, lymphoma

ACTIVATED CHARCOAL—CONTRAINDICATIONS:

CHARCOAL FLAME!

C austics (ie Corrosives)-- cause tissue injury by a chemical reaction— generally broken down into acid and alkaline ingestions

H ydrocarbons

A irway unprotected

R igoring (seizures)

C yanide

O bstruction (mechanical bowel)

A mmonia

L ithium

F lammables (gasoline), Fe (iron)

L ye

A lcohol

M ethanol, Metals

E lectrolytes (K+)

ACUTE MESENTERIC ISCHEMIA: A GHOST

   A nion gap 2° to lactic acidosis; ↑WBC

   G as in the portal vein often noted radiographically

   H eart disease & A fib are common precipitants → emboli to the SMA (superior mesenteric artery)→ ischemia→gangrene; comorbid abdominal vascular thrombosis is a less frequent presentation.

   O ut of proportion to the exam—how the pain is commonly described

   S urgical resection (immediate) of the diseased bowel segment is recommended; Shock (can look like '*a ghost*' !)

   T humbprinting (2° thick, edematous bowel wall); A/F levels may be seen

ALLOPURINOL TOXICITIES: FREE as in "FREE Gout" (but don't Freakout on the test!)…

   F ever

   R ash—Erythematous, desquamating; Renal insufficiency

   E os ↑

   E levated LFTs

ALLOPURINOL—INDICATIONS: SORE MTP

   S tones

   O verproduction of uric acid

   R enal disease (insufficiency/ urate nephropathy)

   E lderly

   M ultiple gouty attacks (≥4 attacks per year)

   T ophaceous gout; Tumor lysis syndrome as cause of hyperuricemia

   P olyarticular disease

ADRENOCORTICAL FAILURE

CAUSES OF ↓ ALDO FOR THE BOARDS...

> <u>1° FAILURE (ADDISON'S Disease)</u>—*these patients have <u>hyperreninemic hypoaldosteronism.</u>*
> a) *Autoimmune is the <u>#1 cause</u>*
> b) TB; fungal disorders
> c) Malignancy

✪ *Waterhouse-Friederickson Syndrome (bilateral adrenal hemorrhage) 2° to sepsis (e.g. meningococcal)*, trauma, anticoagulants--#2 cause in the US.

> <u>2° FAILURE (MOST PATIENTS)</u>
>
> a) *Prolonged steroid use* (suppresses ACTH)--<u>#1 cause</u> of 2° failure
> b) Following removal of adrenal tumor—may take up to 1 year for the HPA axis to recover.
> c) NSAIDs
> d) ACE inhibitors

✪ Frequent association with antithyroid antibodies in autoimmune Addison's.

✪ <u>**THE TREATMENT DIFFERS FOR 1° VS 2° ADRENOCORTICAL FAILURE**</u>:

> ☞ 1°→Glucocorticoid (hydrocortisone) + Mineralcorticoid therapy (fludrocortisone)
>
> ☞ 2°→Glucocorticoid only

✪ <u>**DISTINGUISHING FACTORS**</u> in Primary vs. Secondary/Tertiary adrenal insufficiency:

PRIMARY	SECONDARY/TERTIARY
Associated with **hyperpigmentation**	No hyperpigmentation
Mineralcorticoid and liberal salt intake important in management	Mineralcorticoid secretion intact
↑**ACTH**	↓ACTH

ALPHA-1 ANTITRYPSIN DEFICIENCY: **ABE'S CHEST**

A <u>ugmentation</u> (IV replacement) therapy of alpha 1-antitrypsin (AAT; Prolastin®) <u>at levels of AAT < 11 µmol/L (corresponding to 80 mg/dL</u>), below which there is insufficient AAT to protect the lung.

B <u>ases</u> show more severe emphysema

E lastase, a destructive enzyme in the lung, accumulates secondary to this inherited deficiency of AAT, which is an effective inhibitor of the proteolytic enzyme elastase → lung elastin (and therefore the structural integrity of the lung) is compromised.

S uspect Alpha$_1$-ATD in a <u>young former or current smoker with or without a family history of lung disease, and with an obstructive pattern on spirometry</u>.

C aucasians, usually of Northern European descent, but is also occasionally found in patients of Hispanic origin

H <u>epatitis / cirrhosis</u>

E mphysema: The disease develops rapidly in smokers and leads to emphysema 10 to 15 years earlier than in nonaffected smokers. The average age emphysema presents in those with AAT deficiency is the mid-forties.

S kin disease — panniculitis, characterized by inflammatory lesions of the skin, is the major dermatologic manifestation of AAT deficiency

T ransplanting the liver, reserved for patients with end-stage hepatic disease, has the additional advantage of correcting the AAT deficiency, because the healthy donor liver produces, secretes, and thereby restores the normal levels of AAT.

ALZHEIMER'S DISEASE: WARNING SIGNS // DRUGS:

"OPTIMAL CARE"

WARNING SIGNS FOR EARLY / OPTIMAL RECOGNITION OF ALZHEIMER'S DISEASE: OPTIMAL

O rientation poor

P ersonality changes

T ask performance poor

I nitiative, loss of

M emory loss; Mood changes; Misplacing things

A bstract thinking poor

L anguage problems (trouble finding the right words; word substitution)

4 DRUGS COMMONLY USED FOR TREATING ALZHEIMER'S: CARE

C ognex® (tacrine)

A ricept ® (donepezil)

R eminyl ® (galantamine)

E xelon ® (rivastigmine)

AMEBIC LIVER ABSCESS*

➤ ***Normal LFTs***, usually.
➤ ***Single*** abscess seen in 70% of cases; the fluid on aspiration has been said to resemble "chocolate syrup" or "anchovy paste".
➤ ***Males*** affected in 80% of cases
➤ ***Right*** lobe effected in 90% of cases

*   You can ***remember these*** by recalling, **"Ame is looking for a normal, single, male, Mr. Right"!**

POTENTIAL TOXICITIES OF AMIODARONE INCLUDE:

PHOTO (as in PHOTOsensitivity / PHOTOphobia—see below)

P ulmonary fibrosis (✓ PFTs)

Potentiates warfarin, digoxin, and quinidine, all of which, when used simultaneously, should be decreased by 50%, to avoid toxicity

Prolongs PR, QRS, and most importantly QT, esp in combination with IA antiarrhythmics (quinidine, procainamide, disopyramide)

Peripheral neuropathy

H epatitis (✓ LFTs)

Hypotension is the most common adverse effect occurring with intravenous amiodarone therapy

Heart: bradycardia; AV block (esp w/ beta-blockers or calcium channel blockers)

O cular toxicities: corneal deposits and halo vision being the most common; The most serious, albeit rare, complication is optic Neuritis (discontinuation of amiodarone is required if it occurs); PHOTOphobia

T hyroid dysfunction, hypo or hyper (✓ TFTs)

O thers: CNS: Ataxia, paresthesias, peripheral polyneuropathy, sleep disturbance, impaired memory, and tremor; GI: Nausea, anorexia, constipation; Skin: blue discoloration; PHOTOSensitivity

AML, TYPE 3 (M3)—KEY FEATURES OR ☞ D.A.T.A.

D IC—important association

A uer rods—an important sign, which, when seen, often points to the diagnosis of M3, a potentially curable AML with ATRA (all-transretinoic acid)

T 15,17 translocation—renders PML highly sensitive to & potentially curable with all-transretinoic acid

A TRA

AMYLOIDOSIS: <u>AA vs. AL</u>: <u>WHICH IS WHICH?</u>

Amyloidosis can generally be divided into systemic, β2-microglobulin type (associated with long-term hemodialysis, usually with cuprophane membranes), and localized amyloidosis. Systemic amyloidosis can be further divided into primary (1°), secondary 2°, and familial variants. **<u>1°</u>** is associated with B-cell or <u>plasma cell neoplasms</u> (*multiple myeloma* is classic) and the protein seen are referred to as "**<u>AL</u>**" ('L' for "Light" chains). **<u>2°</u>** amyloidosis is associated with <u>chronic illnesses</u>, such as TB, RA, and osteomyelitis, ankylosing spondylitis, cystic fibrosis, etc), but also with a number of <u>neoplasms too</u> (particularly renal cell carcinoma and Hodgkin's disease). The protein seen is "**<u>AA</u>**". 1° and 2° systemic amyloidoses are often confused. One easy way to remember what goes with what is to remember "AA" also stands for "Alcoholics Anonymous" since alcohol is also a chronic disease. Another "built-in" mnemonic to take note of is simply that "AA" has **2** A's, and therefore is **2°**.

β2-MICROGLOBULIN VARIANT OF AMYLOIDOSIS: Important Features/Associations:

C.L.A.P. *(When you see this one on your exam, the first thing to do would <u>B2 CLAP</u>)...*

    C arpal tunnel syndrome;   <u>Cystic bone lesions</u>
    L ong-term dialysis
    A rthropathy
    P athologic fractures

IMPORTANT ANCA's YOU NEED TO KNOW:

    <u>WE</u>GENER'S granulomatosis: **<u>c-AN</u>CA** (Remember, "Yes, **<u>WE</u>** **<u>c-AN</u>**")

    GOOD**P**ASTURE'S disease → **p-ANCA**

    Polyarteritis Nodosa (PAN) → **p-AN**

ANEMIA OF **C**HRONIC DISEASE

- ➤ A hypoproliferative anemia in which red cell precursors are deficient in their uptake and utilization of iron.

- ➤ It is commonly said that ACD is **associated with** the <u>**3C's**</u>: **C**hronic infections (e.g., osteomyelitis); **C**onnective tissue diseases (e.g., rheumatoid arthritis and SLE); and **C**arcinomas

MACROCYTIC ANEMIAS: BIG BERTHA'S <u>or</u> B. FRESH !

B 12 deficiency

E thanol

R eticulocytosis (secondary to blood loss or hemolysis)

T oxic drugs: eg hydroxyurea, zidovidine, AraC, methotrexate, azathioprine, 6-MP

H ypothyroidism; Hepatic disease

A nemia 2° folate   deficiency

S ideroblastosis

or …

B 12 deficiency

F olate deficiency

R eticulocytosis

E thanol

S ideroblastosis

H ypothyroidism

HYPOCHROMIC, <u>MIC</u>ROCYTIC ANEMIAS:

"A L.I.T. Mic" (as in "a light microscope")

A nemia of Chronic Disease

L ead poisoning

I ron deficiency

T halassemia, Thyroid ↓

NORMOCYTIC, NORMOCHROMIC: *Losing it, Lysing, Low production*

➢ **L**osing it: Acute hemorrhage

➢ **L**ysing it: Acute hemolysis (eg HUS, TTP)

➢ **L**ow production: Aplastic anemia; pure RBC aplasia; myelofibrosis; CRF*

* Erythropoiesis is ↓ in CRF, usually secondary to the effects of retained toxins on the bone marrow as well as to diminished endogenous epo levels by the diseased kidneys.

ANION GAP = [Na - (HCO3 + Cl) = 8-12] :

Causes of High Anion Gap (>12) metabolic acidosis: *K-U-S-S-M-A-U-L* (Ketoacidosis; Uremia; Starvation; Salicylates; Methanol; Alkali loss; Unusual chemicals; Lactate) ; may use in combination with *C--M-U-D P-I-L-E-S* (Cyanide; Methanol; Uremia; DKA; Paraldehyde/Propylene glycol; INH/Iron; Lactate; Ethylene Glycol; Strychnine/Salicylates/Starvation.)

SUMMARY OF KEY FEATURES OF ANKYLOSING SPONDYLITIS:

A.S. M.E.M.O.R.I.E.S.

A ortic Insufficiency

S acroiliitis/Seronegative (neg rheumatoid factor) Spondyloarthropathy (A.S is usually HLA-B27 +)

M orning back stiffness

E nthesopathic involvement
        a) Plantar fasciitis
        b) Achilles tendinitis
        c) Costochondritis

M ales > females; young male is the typical patient on an exam (onset between 15-40yo)

O cular disease → Acute anterior uveitis — Uveitis is the most common extraarticular complication of AS, occurring in 25 to 40 percent of patients;

R educed range of motion of the low back, and Reduced chest expansion (see above) are 2 key physical exam findings

I mproves with exercise or activity; Insidious onset

E rosions & …

S yndesmophytes are 2 key radiographic findings; syndesmophytes account for the "bamboo spine" appearance radiographically

RADIOGRAPHIC FINDINGS IN ANKYLOSING SPONDYLITIS:

"Cover all your B.A.S.E.S."…

B amboo spine

A nkylosis of joints; Atlantoaxial-axial subluxation—can lead to cord compression

S acroiliitis (bilateral, symmetric)

E rosions

S yndesmophytes

Additional points:
- ➢ Fracture of ankylosed spines — Patients with ankylosed spines can develop fracture on mild trauma. The most common site is at the C5-C6 interspace → can lead to cord compression
- ➢ Many patients with AS have restriction in chest expansion due to costovertebral rigidity
- ➢ DISH ('Diffuse Idiopathic Skeletal Hyperostosis', *a form of 1°osteoarthritis)* can confuse radiographically

ANTIARRHYTHMICS, CLASS III VAUGHN-WILLIAMS MEMBERS: BASIC

B retylium
A miodarone
S otalol
I butilide
C ompletes the mnemonic!

ANTICHOLINERGIC SYNDROME (Atropine; TCA's; Antipsychotics; Anthistamines; some Parkinson's meds)

Presentation—Dry skin and mucous membranes; hyperthermia; flushing; tachycardia; HTN; mydriasis; ↓ salivation and sweating; ileus; urinary retention; anxiety/confusion; seizures.

✪ *Mnemonic:* "Dry as a bone; red as a beet; blind as a bat; mad as a hatter; hot as hades"

CHOLINERGIC SYNDROME (Organophosphate poisoning)

Presentation—Essentially the opposite of anticholinergic syndrome, with ↑sweating /salivation/lacrimation; vomiting; diarrhea; miosis; bradycardia; wheezing; muscle cramps; fasciculations; altered mental status.

✪ *Mnemonic*--S-L-U-D-G-E: **S**alivation/sweating; **L**acrimation; **U**rination; **D**efecation; **G**I upset; **E**mesis

ANTIPHOSPHOLIPID ANTIBODY SYNDROME: CLINICAL FEATURES: **VITAL**

V enous thromboses, VDRL (false +)
I ncreased PTT
T hrombocytopenia
A rterial thromboses (TIA, CVA, visceral infarction, extremity gangrene); Abortions (recurrent spontaneous)
L ivedo reticularis

SYMPTOMS AS PROGNOSTICATORS IN AORTIC STENOSIS: **A.S. FAILURE**

A ngina→death within 3-5years (if untreated)
S yncope→death within 2 years
Failure: Dyspnea→death within 1 year /Overt cardiac failure→death within 6mo.

Echocardiographic findings characteristic of **HYPERTROPHIC CARDIOMYOPATHY** ☞ '**SAM ASH**': "**S**ystolic **A**nterior **M**otion of the anterior MV leaflet with **A**symmetric **S**eptal **H**ypertrophy"

KEY FEATURES IN A**PLASTIC** ANEMIA: "**I.D.I.O.T.S.** pay with plastic!"
(& I'm one of them!)

I diopathic = #1 cause
D rugs = #2 cause
I nfections {Hep C (esp) & Hep B } = #3 cause. Parvovirus can induce transient aplastic anemia in nearly all hemolytic conditions, including hereditary spherocytosis, sickle cell, thalassemias, RBC enzyme deficiencies, PNH, and autoimmune hemolysis
O ptions for treatment include: immunosuppression with cyclosporine + steroids, BMT, or ATG (anti-thymocyte globulin; if older than 45-50 and no HLA-match). BMT carries a 65% success rate in young patients. Remember, mortality is 80% at 2 years if goes untreated.
T ransfusions—take special care! If transfusions are needed, select nonrelated donors and use leuk-depleted PRBCs and single-donor platelets. Family members should not be transfusion donors since they are more likely to sensitize the patient to minor HLA antigens present in the donor, but absent in the patient.
S tem cell defect leads to pancytopenia/a hypocellular marrow

ARGYLL-ROBERTSON PUPILS

> ➢ A feature of tertiary <u>syphilis</u>, but may also be seen in <u>diabetes</u>.
> ➢ Usually bilateral
> ➢ Argyll Robertson pupils are small, irregular and unresponsive to light, but they show an intact near response if the patient's visual acuity is intact.
> ➢ Also known as the **"PROSTITUTE'S PUPIL"** because it **"accommodates but does not react."**

ARTHRITIDES/ARTHRITIS—MAJOR CAUSES OF JOINT PAIN: CHRISTO!

C PPD (Pseudogout[1]), Charcot's joints, Crystals (!)

H emarthroses

R A

I nfections (eg HIV, parvovirus, Lyme, TB, brucellosis, GC, etc)

S LE, Sjogrens syndrome, Scleroderma, Systemic vasculitis, Still's disease, Spondyloarthropathies (Psoriatic, Ankylosing Spondylitis, Reiter's, Enteropathic arthritides)

T rauma

O steoarthritis

> 1. Uric acid crystals are <u>negatively birifringent, as opposed to</u> **P**seudogout, which is **P**ositively birifringent under polarized light microscopy.

CAUSES of AFIB: PIRATE SHIP

P ericarditis

I schemia

R heumatic heart disease

A trial myxoma

T hyrotoxicity

E thanol

S ick Sinus Syndrome

H TN (#1 cause)

I diopathic (eg Lone AFib)

P E

AUSTIN-FLINT & GRAHAM-STEEL MURMURS: AI **&** MS

1. **A**ustin-Fl**I**nt murmur (regurgitant jet in severe **AI** encroaches on the anterior leaflet of the mitral valve creating a relative mitral stenosis)

2. *Graha**M**-**S**teel murmur* (severe **MS** + Pulm HTN→ this PI murmur)

AUTOIMMUNE HEPATITIS: GAY LASS

G amma globulins (serum) elevated

A NA, ASMA, ANCA, anti-LKM

Y oung *women*, primarily; average 10-20 yo

L KM, (anti-LKM autoantibodies = anti-liver-kidney-microsomal antibodies)

A utoimmune diseases (additional) are commonly associated: Diseases commonly seen with autoimmune hepatitis include hemolytic anemia, idiopathic thrombocytopenic purpura, type 1 diabetes mellitus, thyroiditis, Arthralgias; Asymptomatic disease and Acute hepatitis are the most common presentations; Azathioprine commonly used in conjunction with corticosteroids (below) in mgmt

S oluble liver antigen; ASMA = anti-Smooth muscle Ab)

S teroids ± azathioprine

AVASCULAR (ASEPTIC) NECROSIS: **GERIATRIC HIPS**

G aucher's disease

E thanol abuse

R adiation

I ntravascular coagulation

A rthropathy, urate (gout)

T rauma (fractures, dislocation); Thrombophlebitis

R enal transplantation; also CRF

I diopathic

C igarette smoking

H emoglobinopathies (sickle cell disease)

I ncreased lipid disorders

P ancreatitis, Pregnancy

S teroid use, chronic; SLE

SITE OF ACTION FROM PRE- TO POST-SYNAPTIC: *Remember* **(B→O→M)**

Botulin → PREsynaptic

Organophosphate poisoning → SYNAPTIC

Myasthenia Gravis → POSTsynaptic

BABESIOSIS: **ASHEN TICK !** *{also helps you recall the two most important elements in this disease: the anemia ("ashen") and the vector ("tick") respectively}*

A splenic or immunocompromised pts → can see overwhelming infection; healthy individuals → usually a mild illness and recover on their own

S ymptoms: It causes primarily flu-like symptoms (fever, chills, fatigue, headache, muscle pain); but can also see abdom pain, dark urine, photophobia, conjunctival injection, sore throat, and cough.

H ematologically, may see → Hemolytic anemia, ↓ haptoglobin, ↑ retic count, normal to ↑ WBC, ↓ platelets, + direct Coombs test, petechiae/ecchymoses, HSM; also may see ↑ BUN/Cr

E xchange transfusion — Exchange transfusion is often used as adjunctive therapy to clindamycin + quinine in selected patients (see below)

N E (northeast) coastal areas (Nantucket, Martha's Vineyard, Cape Cod, Rhode Island, Eastern Long Island, Shelter Island, Fire Island; and CT) and Wisconsin.

T hick and thin smears reveal a "malaria-like" protozoa on —Babesia; in RBC they are often located peripherally, thus commonly mistaken for P. falciparum, esp the ring forms of P. falciparum; however, the brown pigment deposits are seen in P. Falciparum only and Babesiosis may reveal characteristic "tetrads (the parent and "daughter" cells).

I xodes Scapularis / I. Dammini ticks (which also transmit Lyme disease to humans from rodents) ingest Babesia while feeding on rodents and cattle whose erythrocytes have been infected with Babesia, and multiply within the tick's gut wall→tick bites human.

C linda + quinine; ± exchange transfusions

K inds of situations appropriate for exchange transfusion:

✓ Immunodeficiency such as HIV
✓ Severe hemolysis
✓ B. divergens infection (more common in Europe; B. microti for U.S.)
✓ High-level parasitemia (>10 percent)

BACK PAIN—CAUSES: **SADISM**

S tones (nephrolithiasis); Spondylosis

A bdominal pain (eg pancreatitis); Aortic aneurysms

D egeneration (osteoarthritis, spondylosis, osteoporosis); Dissection

I nfection (eg osteomyelitis, epidural abscess, Pott's disease, prostatitis, pyelonephritis, PID); Injury (trauma)

S pondylitis/Spondyloarthropathies; Scoliosis; Strain; Shingles

M etastases; Multiple myeloma

BEHCET'S SYNDROME: **BEHCET'S**

B 5 is an important HLA association (HLA B5), esp when colitis is seen (30% of cases)

E Nodosum

H istopathology: vasculitis, usually leucocytoclastic vasculitis; Hematologic findings: deficiencies of iron, folic acid or vitamin B12 seen in 10%-20% of cases

C olitis in 30%; CNS disease also in 30% (aseptic meningitis, TIA-like episodes; cranial nerve palsies)

E thnicity: more commonly affects individuals from: Mediterranean countries; Middle Eastern countries; China; Korea; and Japan. Eyes: esp. uveitis and conjunctivitis; Epithelial ulcers (orogenital)

T hrombophlebitis also in approx 30%

S pondylitis/Sacroiliitis

BEHCET'S DISEASE-- CLINICAL SPECTRUM: CUT OPENS

C olitis (30%); associated with HLA-B5; clinically overlaps with IBD

U lcers (aphthous oral; genital)

T hrombophlebitis (30%)

O cular disease—occurs in 80%; more common in HLA B5 and Japanese men; eg uveitis

P athergy test-- *Positive pathergy test*: physician-placed oblique insertion of a 20-gauge needle under sterile conditions produces an inflammatory pustule at 24-48 h).

E nodosum (F>M; assoc'd with non-deforming arthritis); occur in 80%

N eurologic disease (30%) (Aseptic meningitis TIA-like episodes cranial nerve palsies)

S pondylits, sacroiliitis; when present, linked to HLA-B27

Oligoarthritis (1/2 of patients; non-erosive, asymmetric; nondeforming)

BEHCET'S SYNDROME—DIAGNOSTIC SIGNS: CUTE SPECS

C olitis in 30%--HLA B5 association

U lcers (oral/genital)

T hrombophlebitis in 30%

E Nodosum

S pondylitis/Sacroiliitis

P athergy test (i/d saline injection)

E ye disease (eg uveitis)

C NS disease also in 30% (aseptic meningitis, TIA-like episodes; cranial nerve palsies)

S kin lesions

BLEEDING TIME– KEY CAUSES: ADD 'M UP

A spirin/NSAIDs; Afibrinogenemia
D IC
D efects of platelet aggregation (eg VWD ; Bernard-Soulier; Glanzmann's)

M yeloproliferative disorders

U remia (defective platelet release)
P araproteinemias

BLOODY DIARRHEA or FECAL LEUKOCYTES: BACTERIAL CAUSES

"YE³S², Can Cause!"

Y ersinia
E ntameba histolytica; Enteroinvasive E. Coli; E. Coli 0157H7
S almonella; Shigella

C ampylobacter jejuni
C. diff colitis (5% of cases present this way)

BOERHAAVE'S SYNDROME: DAMN PERFS!

D ilatation of esophageal strictures & other esophageal medical procedures account for over one-half of all perforations

A lcoholism or heavy drinking is present in 40 percent. Similar to Mallory-Weiss, it often follows violent retching, as after an alcoholic binge

M ediastinal air; Management/Treatment: primary surgical repair of the ruptured esophagus, mediastinal debridement, and pleural drainage. Continuous NG suction, IV broad-spectrum antibiotics, and TPN.

N efarious: Diagnosis + surgery within 24 hours yields a 75% survival, which drops to 50% after a 24-hour delay and 10% after 48 hours. Normal CXR in 10%. The most common finding is a unilateral effusion, usually on the left, since most perfs occur in the left posterior aspect of the esophagus.

P UD history in approx 40%; Pneumomediastinum seen in 20% may cause a crackling sound upon chest auscultation, known as the Hamman crunch.

E xtravasation of contrast material after water-soluble contrast esophagram (Gastrograffin®) is confirmatory and reveals the location and extent of the perf with a 90% sensitivity.

R etching, violent precipitates most non-procedure-related esophageal perforations

F ever, and shock

S igns & Symptoms: odynophagia, tachypnea, dyspnea, cyanosis, excruciating retrosternal chest and upper abdominal sain; Subcutaneous emphysema

BOTULISM Complications: **6 D**'s

Eyes   →   **D** ilated, fixed pupil
              D iplopia
Tongue →   **D** ysarthria
              D ysphagia
              D ry tongue
And… →   **D** escending paralysis

BRONCHIECTASIS—CAUSES: **ASCERTAIN RISK**

A llergic Bronchopulmonary Aspergillosis (ABPA)
S taphylococcal pneumonia
C ystic fibrosis; corrosive chemical injury (acids/alkali)
E osinophilia, pulmonary
R eflux, (chronic aspiration)
T B
A irway obstructions, chronic
I mmotile cilia syndrome
N ecrotizing pneumonia

R are diseases, eg Young's syndrome and yellow nails syndrome
I mmunodeficiencies (eg hypogammaglobulinemia)
S treptococcal pneumonia
K artagener's syndrome

BRUCELLOSIS: HALF-ASSED

H igh-risk groups → slaughterhouse workers/meat packers/butchers/wool & hide workers—*who sometimes do a 'half-assed' job*; farmers; dairymen; livestock handlers; veterinary surgeons; shepherds; Headache
A rthralgias
L ymphadenopathy, and occasionally hepatosplenomegaly; Lower back pain
F ever/FUO

A cquisition via *aerosolization* from infected animal tissues is much less common than acquiring it via *ingestion* (most cases) of unpasteurized sheep/goat milk or cheese.
S acroiliitis
S low growing in cultures; therefore can get false positives. Cultures generally become positive between 7 and 21 days but may take up to 35 days. So, if you suspect it, ask the lab to hang on to the cultures for a longer period.
E pididymoorchitis; Endocarditis
D oxycycline + (streptomycin or rifampin); Dry cough & pleuritic chest pain; Diagnosis: Cultures of blood or other sites, especially bone marrow or liver biopsy specimens; also serum agglutination and ELISA important in diagnosis.

BUERGER'S DISEASE: SURG TIPS

S egmental thrombosing vasculitis (path)
U lcers, chronic
R aynaud's phenomenon
G angrene; Gender (M>F)

T hromboangiitis obliterans (path)
I nstep claudication; Infarction, digital
P ain, even at rest
S uperficial nodular phlebitis

CARCINOMAS THAT METASTASIZE TO BONE:

"These Kinds Metastasize T.O. Bone—Poor Lad !"

T hyroid
K idney
M elanoma
T esticular
O varian
B reast
P arathyroid
L ung, Lymphoma

CAPLAN SYNDROME—KEY FEATURES: CAPLaN

C oal worker pneumoconiosis; cavitation leading to hemoptysis and infection
A rthritis
P leural effusion; pneumothorax; pleuro/broncho fistula
L ow flow (mild obstructive lung disease)
A nd…
N odules, pulmonary

CARDIAC SYNDROME X: MAIN CLINICAL FEATURES: MANAGE

M icrovascular angina in some patients
A typical features of chest pain (e.g. prolonged episodes, poor response to sublingual nitrates)
Antianginals ineffective in approximately 50% of patients
N egative stress echo; Normal coronary angiogram
Not to be confused with the other Syndrome X from endocrinology
A bnormal pain perception in many patients
G ood prognosis overall
E xercise-induced chest pain, so + EST

CLINICAL MANIFESTATIONS OF CARDIAC TAMPONADE: **TAPPED HER**

T achycardia
A ttenuated "y" descent
P ulsus paradoxus*; Pulse pressure narrow
P aradoxical rise in JVD on inspiration (Kussmaul's sign)
E lectrical alternans; Equalization of Pressures
D istant heart sounds

H ypotension
E levated JVD
R apid "x" descent

* In pulsus paradoxus, the decrease in systolic arterial pressure that normally accompanies the reduction in arterial pulse amplitude during inspiration is accentuated (> 10 mmHg). The differential diagnosis for pulsus paradoxus includes pericardial tamponade, constrictive pericarditis, restrictive cardiomyopathy, COPD (exacerbation), asthma (exacerbation), superior vena cava obstruction, pulmonary embolus, hypovolemic shock, pregnancy, and obesity.

IMPORTANT CAUSES OF CARDIOGENIC SHOCK FOLLOWING ACUTE MI:

PAL FITS

P apillary muscle rupture (apical <u>holosystolic murmur</u>; often associated with a <u>thrill</u>; bedside echo a simple way to differentiate this from VSD)→IABP
A neurysm, LV—seen in anterior MIs, another reason for warfarin x 3-6 mo post-MI; surgery for clinically significant decreases in cardiac output
L V Wipeout (Massive MI with 2° loss of ≥ 40% of LV)→IABP

F ree wall rupture → nearly always fatal
I nfarction, RV→give IV fluids
T amponade (free wall rupture can lead also lead to tamponade) → pericardiocentesis
S eptal defect (ventricular) (<u>holosystolic murmur</u> with parasternal <u>thrill</u> typical)→IABP (intra-aortic balloon pump)

ST <u>DEPRESSION</u>—CAUSES: **MED SLIP** (when you slip, you fall <u>*down*</u>)

M VP

E mbolism (PE)

D ilated cardiomyopathy, Digoxin toxicity (also quinidine)

S ubendocardial ischemia or infarct, Shock

L V enlargement with strain

I nferior wall MI reciprocal ST depression, Intracranial hemorrhage

P otassium loss

CELIAC SPRUE (GLUTEN SENSITIVE ENTEROPATHY): **I HOARD GAS**

I ron deficiency anemia, esp (classically) when unresponsive to oral iron

H owell-Jolly bodies on peripheral blood smear; secondary <u>H</u>yperparathyroidism (secondary) caused by vitamin D deficiency

O steomalacia and <u>O</u>steoporosis (2° to ↓ vit D and calcium absorption)

A void → Barley Rye Oats Wheat (these should raise your "**BROW**") Rice, corn, & soybean are fine; <u>A</u>rthritis; <u>A</u>taxia

R BC folate ↓seen in 70%

D ermatitis Herpetiformis—classic rash of celiac disease; extraintestinal manifestation of celiac sprue; a highly pruritic, bullous rash with a predilection for the extensor surfaces

G luten-free diet with symptomatic resolution is the most definitive diagnosis (ie even over biopsy, esp for the boards); <u>G</u>rowth retardation/weight loss; <u>GI</u> upset, persistent, non-specific

A utoAbs may be seen: + Anti-endomysial Ab; + Anti-gliadin Ab; + Anti-reticulin Ab; <u>A</u>nemia due to folate/iron/B12 defiencies

S teatorrhea and flatulence (gas-hoarding!)

CEREBRAL ANEURYSMS-- WHICH MEDICAL CONDITIONS PREDISPOSE ?

"SEARCH ME !"

S ubacute Bacterial Endocarditis
Secondary HTN (selected): eg fibromuscular dysplasia, pheochromocytoma; aortic coarctation)
SLE; Sickle cell disease
Small/medium/large vessel vasculitides
E hlers-Danlos Syndrome (& pseudoxanthoma elasticum)
A ortic Coarctation; AVMs; Alpha$_1$-antitrypsin deficiency
R enal Artery Stenosis due to FMD (fibromuscular dysplasia)
C ystic Kidney Disease (ADPKD); Carcinoma (intracranial tumor)
H ead trauma; Hereditary Hemorrhagic Telangiectasia (HHT)

M odifiable risk factors: **CHAOS**

    C holesterol ↑; Cocaine use
    H TN (essential)
    A ge over 50 years; Alcohol
    O ral contraceptives
    S moking, current

E mboli

HEMATOLOGIC DISEASES ASSOCIATED WITH CEREBRAL INFARCTION:

SLEPT W/ M.e

S ickle cell disease
L eukemia
E ssential thrombocythemia
P Vera
T TP

W aldenstrom's macroglobulinemia

M ultiple myeloma and other hyperviscosity syndromes

CHARCOT'S JOINTS—COMMON DISORDERS PREDISPOSING: STOMPED!

S yringomyelia

T abes dorsalis (/Tertiary syphilis)

O ther conditions causing disease or injury to the spinal cord

M ultiple Sclerosis, Meningomyelocele

P eripheral nerve injury

E thanol

D iabetes mellitus (#1 cause)

CHLAMYDIA PSITTACOSIS: AH! FACTS!

A vian exposure: most patients with psittacosis have a history of contact with birds, e.g. poultry workers cleaning out bird cages, but as many as 3/4^{ths} of patients are simply exposed to through their own pets.

H yponatremia common; Headaches, severe

F ever, abrupt onset

A ST ↑ in nearly half of patients;

C ough, dry; Constitutional symptoms: rigors, sweats, and myalgias

T reatment: Doxycycline and TCN are the drugs of choice; Toxic granulations often noted on peripheral blood smear and diff shows a left shift (total WBC count, however, is usually normal)

S erology via the complement fixation test is the test traditionally used to make the diagnosis. It is the most widely available but unfortunately cannot differentiate among the Chlamydial species. Paired acute and convalescent Sera should be obtained at least two weeks apart, and a fourfold rise in antibody levels is significant.

CHLORIDE-RESISTANT (or Chloride-Unresponsive) METABOLIC ALKALOSES:

"CHLORIDE"

C ongenital hypertrophy of the JG (juxtaglomerular) apparatus → Bartter's syndrome (usually normotensive) hyperaldosteronism

H yperaldosteronism

L iddle syndrome

O verabundance of corticosteroids

R enal artery stenosis

I nadequate (or "Insufficent") magnesium

D eficiency in 11 beta-hydroxylase (Congenital Adrenal Hyperplasia)

R enin-secreting tumors

E xogenous mineralocorticoids

[NOTE: Except for Bartter's, which is normal-to-low BP, the rest are typically associated with ↑BP]

CHRONIC ATROPHIC GASTRITIS ('Nonerosive Gastritis'): TYPES A & B

TYPE **A**		TYPE **B**
Associated with **pernicious**	⟷	*Associated with* **H. Pylori** (& PUD)
Anemia & gastric carcinoids	⟷	H. Pylori **B**acteria is actually responsible!
Body/fundus of stomach	⟷	***Antrum*** of stomach
Serum gastrin ↑	⟷	***Normal*** serum gastrin

- ***Both*** types are associated with ***adenocarcinoma***.

- ***Both*** are usually **asymptomatic**.

- In patients with type B gastritis, eradication of *H. pylori* is generally not recommended in the absence of documented peptic ulcer or MALT lymphoma.

CHRONIC HEPATITIS—IMPORTANT CAUSES: ABCDEF

A utoimmune Hepatitis (✓anti-smooth muscle Ab; anti-LKM; soluble liver Ag);
Alpha-1-antitrypsin deficiency

B iliary cirrhosis (✓ anti-mitochondrial Ab); hepatitis <u>B</u>

C opper excess (*Wilson's* disease → ✓serum/urine/liver copper ↑; ceruloplasmin usually ↓); Hepatitis <u>C</u>; <u>C</u>holangitis, sclerosing

D rugs

E thanol

F e overload (*Hemochromatosis*→ ✓ transferrin saturation

SUPPLEMENTS TO CONSIDER IN CRF: BCDE

B icarbonate

C alcium (e.g. phosphate binders such as calcium carbonate and calcium acetate)

D vitamin

E rythropoietin

CHURG-STRAUSS SYNDROME: CHEAP PORN

C ardiovascular complications-- account for half the mortality in CSS, via acute pericarditis, constrictive pericarditis, heart failure, and MI.
<u>C</u>NS: cerebral hemorrhage and cerebral infarction are also important causes of death.
<u>C</u>orticosteroids yield excellent response

H TN

E osinophilia of >10 % on diff[1]; ↑ blood & tissue eos [a]

A <u>sthma</u>[1]

P aranasal sinus abnormalities[1] (eg polyps)

P- ANCA

O verlap with PAN significant; but think pulmonary involvement more for Churg-Strauss (lungs[b]=#1 organ; skin = #2[c]) *versus* renal and GI involvement more for PAN

R hinitis, allergic

N europathy[1], peripheral (usually mononeuritis multiplex), seen in approx 75 % of patients; if untreated can progress to a polyneuropathy (symmetric or asymmetric).
Negative prognosticators (most significant ones) = GI and cardiac involvement

    [a]   Biopsy containing a blood vessel showing the accumulation of eosinophils in extravascular areas[1]

    [b]   Migratory or transient pulmonary opacities detected radiographically[1]

    [c]   Skin disease: Two-thirds of patients have skin lesions → usually subcutaneous nodules on the extensor surfaces of the arms, hands, and legs. Skin involvement isone of the most common features of the vasculitic phase of CSS.

[1]   4 out of these 6 marked criteria from the ACR (American College of Radiology) yield a sensitivity of 85 percent and a specificity of 99.7 percent for CSS:
NAB PEN:

N europathy (mono or poly)

A sthma (a history of wheezing or the finding of diffuse high pitched wheezes on expiration)

B iopsy containing a blood vessel showing the accumulation of eosinophils in extravascular areas

P ulmonary opacities detected radiographically (migratory or transient)

E osinophilia of >10 percent on differential white blood cell count

N asal/paranasal sinus abnormality

CIRRHOSIS—KEY CAUSES: **WHAT BS !**

W ilson's disease/copper exces
H emochromatosis
A lcoholic hepatitis
　　Autoimmune hepatitis
　　Alpha-1 Antitrypsin deficiency
T ypes B & C viral hepatitis

B iliary cirrhosis
S clerosing cholangitis

CLUBBING #1: **CLUBBING**

C ystic fibrosis; Cirrhosis; Cyanotic heart disease
L ung processes: bronchietasis, abscess, TB cancer, pulmonary fibrosis
U lcerative colitis
B iliary cirrhosis
B acterial endocarditis
I diopathic clubbing; Inherited clubbing
N eurogenic tumors
G raves' disease / thyrotoxicosis; Gastric malignancies

CLUBBING #2—CAUSES: **C5 NAILS** (as in "See 5 nails")

C yanotic heart disease
C ystic Fibrosis
C rohn's disease
C irrhosis
C arditis (endocarditis)

N eoplasm (lung)
A bsorption disorders (GI tract)
I nflammatory Bowel Disease (UC, Crohn's)
L ung diseases (other): bronchiectasis, TB, etc.; Low oxygen states
S arcoidosis

COMA—ETIOLOGIES: VICTIM

V ascular (subdural or subarachnoid hemorrhage; infarction)
I nfection (meningitis/encephalitis)
C ardiovascular (shock, severe HTN)
T rauma, Tumor
I ntoxications (sedatives, alcohol, analgesics, tranquilizers, insulin)
M etabolic

HTN + COMORBID CONDITION ☞ CHOOSE AN ACE INHIBITOR: SHARED
(as in SHARED indications)

S econdary MI and stroke prevention
H ypertensive proteinuria; Heart failure
A cute MI (beta-blockers too)
R enal insufficiency
D iabetes ± proteinuria

HTN + COMORBID CONDITION ☞ BETA-BLOCKERS MAKE AN … IMPACT

I nfarction (MI)--also ACE inhibitors/blockers—see above
M igraine (propranolol classic; also CCBs, eg verapamil)
P reoperative HTN
A Fib/ATach (also CCBs)
A ngina (also CCBs)
C HF (again)
T hyrotoxicosis; Tremors, essential (non-cardioselective beta-blockers, eg propranolol)

HTN + COMORBID CONDITION ☞ CHOOSE A DIURETIC: CIAO !

C HF (again)
I solated systolic HTN in elderly patients (also long-acting CCBs)
A frican-American heritage (esp thiazides)
O steoporosis (esp thiazides)

COMPLICATIONS OF ACUTE *OR* CHRONIC PANCREATITIS:

"P" for Pancreas

P hlegmon—a mass of inflamed pancreatic tissue often containing patchy areas of necrosis

P seudocysts[1]— collections of pancreatic juice enclosed by a wall of fibrous or granulation tissue; resolve spontaneously, usually within weeks

P recipitation of calcium salts leads to hypocalcemia

P ersistent ↑ amylase, abdominal pain & fever point to pancreatic abscess; these *usually* occur 2-4 weeks after the acute episode and MUST be drained!

P leural effusion / ARDS; Pancreatic ascites

P seudoaneurysms of the splanchnic arteries (via mesenteric angiography)

P oor sugar control (diabetes)

P ortal HTN due to splenic vein thrombosis

[1] *Additional Notes On Pancreatic Pseudocysts*:

➢ Seen in approx 15% of cases of acute pancreatitis
➢ 85% are located in the body and tail of the pancreas
➢ They represent collections of tissue, fluid, debris, pancreatic enzymes, and blood which develop over a period of 1 to 4 weeks after the onset of acute pancreatitis.
➢ In contrast to true cysts, pseudocysts do not have an epithelial lining; rather, the walls consist of necrotic tissue, granulation tissue, and fibrous tissue.
➢ Usually resolve spontaneously; however, pseudocysts that are greater than 5 cm in diameter and that persist for longer than 6 weeks should be considered for drainage due to an increased risk of complications.

✪ CONGENITAL ADRENAL HYPERPLASIA

☞ *Must know these clinical associations*…

✪ **17 α hydroxylase deficiency** ⟶ **HTN** (might choose to remember this by "a <u>hyper teen</u>ager" ☞ i.e. **HYPER**tension + seven**TEEN.**

✪ **21-hydroxylase deficiency** ⟶ **VIRILIZATION**; 21-hydroxylase deficiency is the most common (95%) form of CAH; might remember *"becoming a man (virilization) at age 21"*

SYNTHESIS PATHWAYS OF CORTISOL AND TESTOSTERONE :

a thru c = enzymes, from which you should *know for your exam*,

> **a = 17α-hydroxylase**
> **b = 21-hydroxylase**
> **c = 11β-hydroxylase**

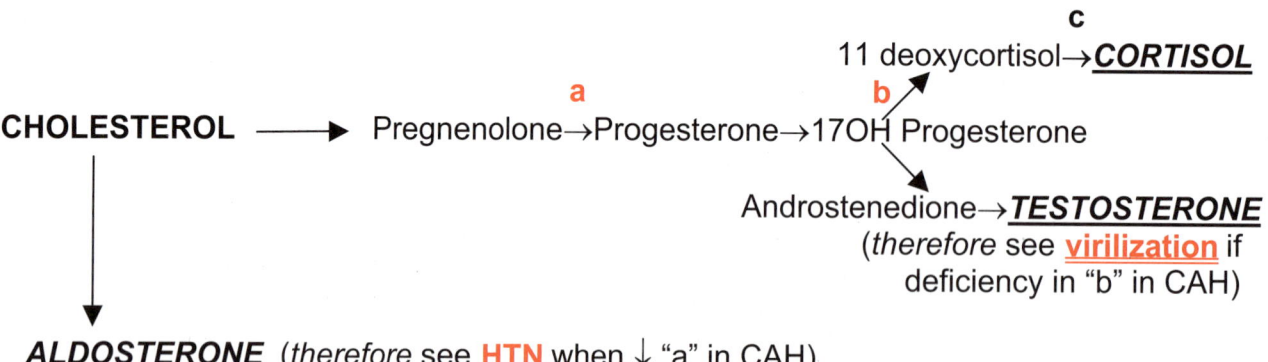

CHOLESTEROL ⟶ Pregnenolone→Progesterone→17OH Progesterone

        c
11 deoxycortisol→***CORTISOL***

Androstenedione→***TESTOSTERONE***
(*therefore* see **virilization** if deficiency in "b" in CAH)

ALDOSTERONE (*therefore* see **HTN** when ↓ "a" in CAH)

COMMON EXAMPLES OF CONTACT DERMATITIS: RE: PLANT (*as in* "Remember to PLANT" *an allergen skin panel*)

R hus (genus of PLANT for poison ivy/poison oak)
E thylenediamine (part of aminophylline)--dyes, fungicides

P araphenylenediamine (hair dyes, fur dyes, chemicals used in photographic work);
Potassium dichromate (cement, leather, household cleaners, bleaches)
L atex (eg gloves, elastic, condomes)
A dhesive dressings
N ickle sulfate (earrings, zippers, hairpins, door handles, silverwork, hair dyes & bleaches, insecticides, fungicides); Nail polish (eg eyelid dermatitis from scratching); Neomycin (a common allergen found in both prescription and non-prescription topical antibiotic creams, ointments, lotions, ear drops, and eye drops. It is also used in combination with other topical antibiotics, topical steroids and in first aid creams.)
T hiuram--rubber products (gloves, tires, rubber shoe soles, waist elastic in underwear/bras), fungicides, insecticides

COOMB'S POSITIVE AUTOIMMUNE HEMOLYSIS:

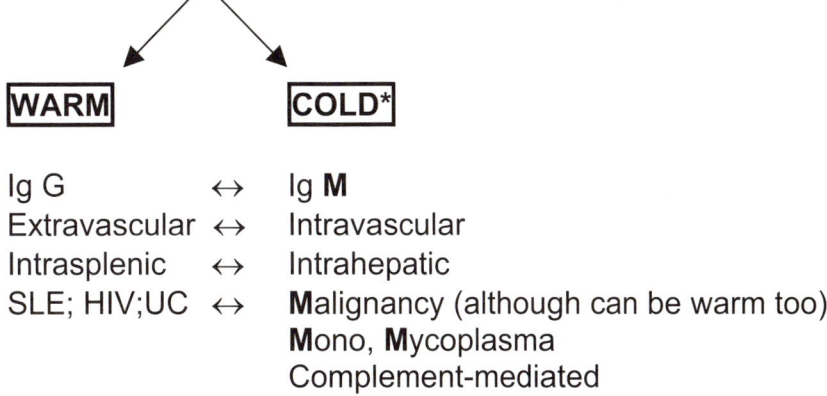

WARM		COLD*
Ig G	↔	Ig **M**
Extravascular	↔	Intravascular
Intrasplenic	↔	Intrahepatic
SLE; HIV;UC	↔	**M**alignancy (although can be warm too), **M**ono, **M**ycoplasma
		Complement-mediated

* One might remember: "**M**mmm, **cold** beer. My **Compliments** to your bar." (beer→intrahepatic)

COMMON CAUSES OF COPD: ABCDE

A sthma—***reversible*** airway obstruction

B ronchitis

C ystic Fibrosis

D ilatation of the bronchi (Bronchiectasis)—***irreversible*** →look for "train-tracking" on the CXR

E mphysema

CREST SYNDROME:

C alcinosis cutis

R aynaud's phenomenon

E sophageal dysmotility

S clerodactyly

T elangietasias

CRYOGLOBULINEMIA: TYPE I: CLINICAL ASSOCIATIONS: I.M.

M onoclonal cryoglobulinemia antibody

M ultiple Myeloma

M GUS (monoclonal gammmopathy of undetermined significance)

M acroglobulinemia (Waldenstrom's)

M alignancies (lymphomas/leukemias)

CRYOGLOBULINEMIA / CRYOGLOBULINS: BASIC POINTS:

➤ Remember, cryoglobulins are *antibodies that precipitate when cooled*; when they do, they yield a <u>leukocytoclastic vasculitis</u>.

➤ Exacerbations of disease activity can, therefore, <u>follow cold exposure</u>

➤ Should be considered a type of vasculitis since the cryoglobulins precipitate in the dermal vessels.

DON'T CONFUSE CRYOGLOBULINS (esp Type I) & COLD AGGLUTININS:
Both are big on "M"s, so don't confuse …
(that is, know 'M *cold* !)

	CRYOGLOBULINEMIA	**COLD AGGLUTININS**
Etiology	**Cryoglobulins** are immunoglobulins that precipitate in the cold—these may be **M**onoclonal (type I) or "**M**ixed" (types II, III)—*vasculitides*	**Cold agglutinins** Ig**M**[1] antibodies vs. RBCs (these are Coomb's + *autoimmune hemolytic anemias*!!)
Associated conditions	➢ **M**alignancy ➢ **M**ultiple myeloma ➢ **M**acroglobulinemia	➢ **M**easles, **M**umps **M**ono **M**ycoplasma [2]
Treatments	➢ Treatment of the primary disease, if any. ➢ Avoidance of cold; ➢ Plasmapheresis ➢ Interferon alfa plus ribavirin (eg Rebetron®) for mixed types associated with chronic Hep C	➢ Treatment of the primary disease, if any. ➢ Avoidance of cold; ➢ Plasmapheresis to physically remove the IgM antibody from the plasma, decreasing the rate of hemolysis; ➢ Cytotoxic agents, particularly cyclophosphamide and chlorambucil, have been given to reduce the production of antibody.

1   *Warm vs Cold Agglutinins*--IgG antibodies generally react with protein antigens on the RBC surface at *body temperature*. For this reason, they are called "warm agglutinins". These account for > 80 % of all cases of autoimmune hemolytic anemias. IgM antibodies generally react with polysaccharide antigens on the red cell surface only at temperatures below that of the core temperature of the body. They are therefore called "cold agglutinins."

2   In mycoplasma pneumoniae, mononucleosis, and other viral diseases, the titer of antibody is usually *too low to cause clinical symptoms*, but its presence is of diagnostic value; only occasionally is hemolysis present.

CRYOGLOBULINEMIA*—Types II & III: **"P's"**—*To help you remember which is which, it works out nicely: M comes before P just as I before II and III.*

P olyclonal cryoglobulinemia antibodies (Type II has monoclonal Ab as well; Type III polyclonal Ab only)

P alpable Purpura

P olyarthralgias

P eripheral neuropathy

P roliferative glomerulonephritis

(Proteinuria/hematuria/hypocomplementemia)

P resence of chronic Hep C (HCV) infection in the majority of patients. In fact, the presence of a high RF titer in patients with purpura but without clinical evidence for rheumatoid arthritis should raise the possibility of HCV infection and cryoglobulinemia. In addition to HCV, other autoimmune disorders are frequently present.

P lasmapheresis-- temporarily lowers the level of globulins, removes the immune complexes, and improves symptoms. However, long-term management should include, if possible, control of the underlying disease that produces the abnormal globulins or immune complexes.

P alpable spleen/liver/lymph nodes (i.e. enlarged)

CUSHING'S SYNDROME: **Steroid M.A.S.O.C.H.I.S.T. !**

S **teroid** psychosis

M oon face, plethora

A cne (monomorphous with few or no comedones)

   Acanthosis nigricans

   Amenorrhea

S triae, bruises

O besity (truncal)

C arbohydrate Intolerance

H TN; Hirsutism;; Hump ('buffalo hump')

I ncreased incidence of tinea versicolor

S mall cell (oat cell) lung ca can give a paraneoplastic Cushing's from ectopic production of ACTH

T erminology: *remember*, Cushing's "*disease*" refers to a pituitary ACTH-producing adenoma; versus "*syndrome*" which refers to adrenal or ectopic production

CUSHING'S DISEASE vs. CUSHING'S SYNDROME

- $2°$ to steroid excess (↑cortisol; opposite of adrenocortical failure!)

- Actually, the *terminology* goes…

   a) Cushing's **Disease**=$2°$ disease at the level of the pituitary; caused by ACTH-producing tumor or hyperplasia.

   b) Cushing's **Syndrome**=$1°$ disease at the level of the adrenal.

✪ CUSHING'S DIFFERENTIAL AND DIAGNOSTICS

DIAGNOSIS:	ACTH:	Suppressible with High Dose (8mg) Dexamethasone (DST) ?
Disease (pituitary level)	↑	Y
Syndrome (adrenal level)	↓	N
Ectopic ACTH (e.g. tumors)	↑	N

The two screening tests for Cushing's includes 24-hour urine collection for free-cortisol and the overnight dexamethasone suppression test (1 mg by mouth at 11 p.m. with measurement of an 8 a.m. cortisol level). **_A 24 hour urine for free cortisol_** *is the* **simplest screen** *for Cushing's syndrome.*

☞ *If results of your screening test are abnormal, then advance to low and high-dose DST for confirmation and etiology…*

✪ DEXAMETHASONE SUPPRESSON TEST (DST) ESSENTIALS:

a) **Overnight** DST is for **_screening_**; aka *(or can do a 24h urine for free cortisol)*

b) **Low-dose** DST is for **_confirmation_**, ie to R/O false positives, such as:

    (1) Estrogen or BCPs or pregnancy
    (2) Simple obesity
    (3) Depression
    (4) Alcoholism
    (5) Hospitalized patients

c) **High-dose** DST is for **_pinpointing_** the exact cause. high dose can pinpoint the dx:
    ☞ Do the high dose test if low dose fails to suppress cortisol
    ☞ If the cortisol **suppresses** to < 5 µg/dl → **Cushing's disease** (pituitary)
    ☞ If not → ectopic ACTH or adrenal tumor

DERMATOLOGY QUICK- LINKS ™

✪ SKIN DISEASE AS A MANIFESTATION OF MALIGNANCY…

1. **Acanthosis nigricans** (not just DM and obesity!)→ GI malignancy, esp gastric, ovarian

2. **Actinic keratosis**→Squamous cell carcinoma
3. **Café au lait spots**→ Von Recklinghausen's disease
4. **Dysplastic nevus**→Malignant melanoma
5. **Epidermal cysts, fibromas, lipomas**→Gardner's syndrome
6. **Flushing, telangiectasias**→Carcinoid tumors
7. **Mucosal hyperpigmentation** (esp. lips)→ Peutz-Jeghers syndrome
8. **Necrolytic erythematous rash**→Glucagonoma

9. **Erythroderma**→ Sezary syndrome (rare variant of cutaneous T-cell lymphoma, aka mycosis fungoides), mycosis fungoides

10. **Dermatomyositis** (esp. steroid-resistant form in adults)→Many types of cancers, esp ovarian/gastric/lung ca.; look for heliotrope rash/Gottron's papules/violaceous erythematous rash

11. **Post-proctoscopic periorbital 'pinch' purpura**→Myeloma with 2° amyloidosis
12. **Acquired ichthyosis**→Hodgkin's Disease

13. **Hirsutism**→PCO (Polycystic Ovary Syndrome); adrenal or ovarian tumors (2° to androgen excess)

14. **Erythema gyratum repens**→Classically associated with breast ca

15. **Sweet's syndrome** (acute febrile neutrophilic dermatosis)→AML; Sweet's syndrome is characterized by painful plaque-forming inflammatory papules and associated with Fever, arthralgias, and peripheral ↑WBC. Note, the fever/arthralgias/splenomegaly/ ↑WBC is similar to Still's Disease

16. **Generalized pruritis**→May be indicative of lymphoma
17. **Tylosis (palmar/plantar keratoderma)**→Esophageal carcinoma
18. **Pemphigus**→Thymoma ± myasthenia gravis
19. **Bullous pemphigoid**→Has not been associated with any underlying malignancy

20. **Ashleef spots**→Tuberous sclerosis (also associated with mental retardation, seizures, and renal angiomyolipomas)

✪ CUTANEOUS MANIFESTATIONS IN INFECTIOUS DISEASE

1. **Keratoderma Blenorrhagicum** (vesicular rash on the palms/soles that crusts)→***Reiter's Syndrome*** (other signs include conjunctivitis, uveitis, urethritis, and arthritis); rash known differently as **Circinate Ballinitis** if affects the glans penis.

2. **Ampicillen (or Amoxicillin) + Infectious Mono (EBV or CMV)**→ Almost all patients develop a morbilliform rash, defined as an exanthematous (viral-like) drug eruption, often mimicking rash of measles.

3. **Measles**→A maculopapular rash that ***spreads from the head down and resolves in the same order*** after approximately 3 days.

4. **Rocky Mt. Spotted Fever (RMSF)**→Erythematous and hemorrhagic macules and papules ***begin peripherally*** (wrists/forearms, ankles) ***and spread centripetally*** to arms, thighs, trunk, face. Fever, H/A, myalgia typically accompany.

5. **Ecthyma Gangrenosum**→ A cellulitis with necrosis related to septic vasculitis. It begins with cutaneous infarction and progresses to large, ulcerated gangrenous lesions. The causative organism is ***Pseudomonas Aeruginosa***; the patient is usually immunocompromised/neutropenic and bacteremia is common.

6. **Impetigo**→***crusted golden-yellow erosions*** which become confluent on the nose, cheeks, chin, and lips 2° to Staph Aureus and Group A Strep (Pyogenes).

7. **Erysipelas**→ Red, painful cellulitis 2° to Staph aureus, but more commonly group A Strep. The margins of the cellulitis are raised, and the borders are sharply demarcated.

8. **Erysipeloid**→A violaceous erythematous cellulitis to the hand 2° to Erysipelothrix rhusiopathiae after handling saltwater fish, shellfish, meat, hides, poultry. (DDx is V. Vulnificus)

9. **Desquamation + Strawberry tongue**→***Scarlet fever*** 2° to Group A Strep; Kawasaki disease may also give a Strawberry tongue + a Desquamating rash.

10. **Purpura Fulminans**→The cutaneous manifestation of DIC or ***acute meningococcemia***; the less fulminant cases of meningococcemia may manifest as a more discrete petechial rash.

11. **Cat Scratch Disease**→caused by ***Bartonella henselae*** (formerly Rochalimaea henselae) and is a ***benign, self-limiting*** infection characterized by a primary skin or conjunctival lesion, following cat scratches or contact with a cat, and subsequent tender regional LN.

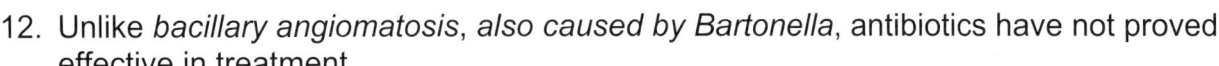

12. Unlike *bacillary angiomatosis, also caused by Bartonella*, antibiotics have not proved effective in treatment.

13. <u>Rosacea</u>—A chronic acneform disorder of the facial pilosebaceous units. ↑ capillary sensitivity to heat results in flushing and ultimately telangiectasia. Long-standing disease with edema and hyperplasia of the skin overlying the nose, cheeks, and forehead leads to **<u>Rhinophyma.</u>**

14. <u>**Pityriasis Versicolor**</u>→A chronic, asymptomatic scaling rash caused by the **hyphal** form of Pityrosporum ovale, characterized by well-demarcated scaling patches with variable hyperpigmentation, usually occurring on the trunk. Diagnosis confirmed by a + KOH prep. **It's other name is Tinea Versicolor**. Treatment is antifungals, like ketoconazole or itraconazole or topical azole creams, selenium sulfide, or propylene glycol.

15. <u>**Pityriasis Rosea**</u>—Distinctive rash that **begins as a "herald patch"**, **usually on the trunk**, followed 1-2 weeks later with a generalized exanthematous eruption that resolves spontaneously after 6 weeks without therapy. More common in the **spring and fall.** May be 2° to picornavirus.

16. <u>**Sporotrichosis**</u>—An ulceronodular dermatosis caused by Sporothrix schenckii, a fungus commonly found in **soil, and usually affecting gardeners**, farmers, florists, lawn workers. Chronic nodular lymphagitis and regional lymphadenitis are concomitant.

17. STD's (chancroid, chancre, etc)→see ID lecture. However, should remember that **among the <u>genital ulcers</u>,** Chancroid, HSV, and Behcet's→ **are PAINFUL;** Syphilis (Syphi<u>LESS</u>), LGV, and Granuloma Inguinale→ **are pain<u>LESS</u>**

✪ SELECTIVE CUTANEOUS DISEASES IN AIDS

1. <u>**Kaposi's sarcoma**</u>—oval papules or purplish plaques on the trunk, extremities, face, mucosa;
2. <u>**Herpes Zoster**</u> (shingles) → VZV
3. <u>**Oral hairy leukoplakia**</u> → <u>EBV</u> and usually seen in advanced AIDS. (This is **<u>not the same as</u>** "<u>oral leukoplakia</u>", which is related to <u>HPV, smoking, smokeless tobacco, alcohol, and syphilis</u>. Candida can invade oral leukoplakia secondarily, and it is considered a premalignant lesion for squamous cell ca)
4. <u>**Molluscum contagiosum**</u> → Discrete, solid, skin-colored papules that are only 1-2 mm in diameter, have central umbilication
5. <u>**Bacillary angiomatosis**</u> (vascular papules or nodules caused by Bartonella (Rochalimaea) henselae and quintana and transmitted by cats or ticks)→Erythromycins or Doxycycline for rx.

✪ CUTANEOUS SIGNS OF SYSTEMIC DISEASE

1. **Pyoderma Gangrenosum**→ *IBD* (UC> Crohn's); *Rheumatoid Arthritis*

2. **Heliotrope rash** (periorbital discoloration)→*Dermatomyositis*

3. **Lupus Pernio** (erythematous swelling of the nose) and Erythema Nodosum→*sarcoidosis*

4. **E. Nodosum** + Fever + arthralgias + bilateral hilar LN → **Löfgren's Syndrome**, with which acute *sarcoidosis* may present; usually a self-limited process of less than 6 month's duration

5. **Pseudoxanthoma elasticum** (yellow xanthomatous papules seen on the abdomen/groin/ neck/axilla→ ↑ risk of CVA, MI, PVD, MVP, angioid streaks in the retina

6. **Ehlers-Danlos syndrome** (skin hyperextensibility + joint hypermobility) →↑ risk of angina, PVD, MVP, GI bleed

7. **Hereditary Hemorrhagic Telangiectasia** (Osler-Weber-Rendu)=cutaneous and mucosal telangiectasias → associated with nosebleeds, GI bleeds, pulmonary AVMs, and CNS angiomas

8. **Acrodermatitis enteropathics** →*Zinc deficiency* ± alopecia, diarrhea

9. **Dermatitis herpetiformis** (immune-mediated bullous disease)→*Celiac disease*

10. **Apthous ulcers**→*Celiac disease; Crohn's disease; Behcet's disease; Reiter's Syndrome; HIV*

11. **Mucosal/Labial hyperpigmentation**→*Peutz-Jeghers syndrome* (no ↑ risk of developing ca)

12. **Erythema Chronicum Migrans**→*Lyme Disease*

13. **C.R.E.S.T. (variant of scleroderma)** = Calcinosis cutis; Raynaud's phenomenon; Esophageal dysmotility; Sclerodactyly; and Telangiectasias

14. **Livido Reticularis**; this is a mottled bluish (livid) discoloration of the skin that looks like a net. It is not a diagnosis per se, but more a reaction pattern to vasculitis syndromes, drugs, atheroemboli. Causes include *SLE, polyarteritis nodosa, and*

cholesterol embolization. Treatment options include: alpha blockers, calcium channel blockers, and ACE inhibitors

15. **Morphea** (discrete sclerotic plaques with white shiny center)→*Scleroderma*

16. **Eosinophilic Fasciitis** (tightly bound thickening of skin and underlying tissues)→*Scleroderma*

17. Erythematous macular-papular eruption of trunk/palms/soles after BMT→**GVHD**

18. **Necrobiosis lipoidica diabeticorum** (yellow-brown atrophic telangiectatic plaques on the shins)→*Diabetes Mellitus*

19. **Pretibial Myxedema** (pink- and skin-colored papules, plaques, and nodules, usually occurring on the shins)→Graves' disease. Do not confuse this dermatologic myxedema with the myxedema associated with Hypothyroidism ("Myxedema coma")

20. **Toxic Epidermal Necrolysis and Stevens-Johnson Syndrome**→mucocutaneous usually *drug-induced* skin tenderness and erythema, followed by extensive exfoliation

21. **Janeway lesions**→ Infective endocarditis. *Nontender*, hemorrhagic, infarcted macules and papules on the fingers, palms, soles; they represent septic emboli. While **Osler's nodes** are also seen in infective endocarditis and have a similar distribution, they are, by contrast, *tender* and represent arteriolar intimal proliferation with extension into the capillaries.

22. **SSSS (Staphylococcal Scalded-Skin Syndrome)**-A Staph aureus *toxin-mediated* painful, tender, diffuse erythema that is followed by desquamation and occurring mainly in newborns and infants under 2 yo

23. **Toxic Shock Syndrome**—Similar to SSSS, it is a Staph aureus *toxin-mediated* illness that causes Fever, Hypotension, generalized skin and mucosal erythema, and multisystem failure occurring in menstrual and nonmenstrual patterns

24. **"Salmon-colored"** rash + arthralgias + ↑ WBC + Fever + Splenomegaly→***Still's Disease*** → think…"*RASH*", *that's*: **R**ash, **A**rthralgias, **S**plenomegaly, **H**igh white count and temp.

25. **Cushing's Syndrome**→ "buffalo hump" (fat pad), purple striae (usu. on the abdomen), hirsutism, steroid acne

CYSTIC FIBROSIS: PINK SCHNAPPS

P seudomonas aeruginosa a common cause of recurrent pneumonia

I nfertility (nearly all men and women with CF); azospermia in men

Immotile Cilia Syndrome (Kartagener's syndrome) often mistakenly for CF because of the combination of sinusitis and infertility

N asal polyps (48%)

K lebsiella pneumoniae is another common cause of recurrent pneumonia

S weat Chloride ≥ 60 on pilocarpine iontopheresis on 2 separate occasions

C OPD (bronchiectasis/bronchitis/bronchiolitis); Caucasians esp

H emoptysis (71%); H.flu; Human DNase has been shown to reduce mucus viscosity and promote mucociliary clearance in Cystic Fibrosis, but has not proven effective in other causes of bronchiectasis.

N ail findings (clubbing)

A spergillus (ABPA in 10% of CFers)

P ancreatic insufficiency → malnutrition → weight loss; pancreatic insufficiency also → diabetes

P urulent sputum

S inusitis; Staph aureus (MRSA/MSSA) pneumonia; Steatohepatitis

DERMATOMYOSITIS: SH!T HAPPENS

S ymmetric, proximal muscle weakness

H ands: Gottron's papules (symmetric, nonscaling, violaceous erythematous eruptions seen over the knuckles) are pathognomonic; also: Raynaud's phenomenon and mechanic's hands (roughening and "dirty" hyperpigmentation of the hands associated with xerosis and fissuring; may be seen with various types of myositis)

I ncreased membrane irritability, as noted by the classic triad of EMG findings:
- ✓ Increased insertional activity and spontaneous fibrillations.
- ✓ Abnormal myopathic low amplitude, short–duration polyphasic motor potentials.
- ✓ Bizarre high–frequency discharges

T umors: patients at ↑ risk for **GO CLUB!** : <u>G</u>astric, <u>O</u>vary, <u>C</u>olon, <u>L</u>ung, <u>U</u>terus, <u>B</u>reast)

H eliotrope rash (periorbital)

A ssociations: polymyositis, interstitial pneumonitis, myocardial involvement, and vasulitis

<u>A</u>nti–Jo–1 antibody, the most prevalent myositis–specific antibody (directed against the anti–histidyl–tRNA synthetase), is found in approx. 20 % of cases and is closely associated with interstitial lung disease/pulmonary fibrosis, Raynaud's phenomenon, arthritis, and mechanic's hands. Anti-Jo-1 is also associated with 30% of polymyositis cases;

<u>A</u>nti-Mi-2 antibodies are highly specific for DM but lack sensitivity because only 25% of the patients with DM demonstrate them. They are associated with acute-onset classic DM with the V-shaped and shawl sign (upper back poikiloderma rash) and a relatively good prognosis.

P hotosensitive, erythematous macular dermatitis (the heliotrope/shawl sign, V-of-the-neck distribution/Gottron's papules are all manifestations of this)

P oikiloderma (hypo- and hyperpigmented macular patches)

E levated CK and aldolase during acute phase

N ails: cuticular hypertrophy, periungal telangiectasias, punctate infarcts

S teroids ± azathioprine for management

DIALYSIS INDICATIONS: I HAVE 2 PEE

I ngestions, toxic (eg methanol, ethylene glycol, etc)

H yperkalemia, life-threatening
A cidosis
V olume excess
E dema, refractory pulmonary

2

P ericarditis
E ncephalopathy, uremic
E levated BUN/creat

IMPORTANT CLINICAL ASSOCIATIONS WITH DIC: S.L.O.T.S. [1]

S epsis (neisseria meningitides classic)
L iver disease: advanced cirrhosis; fulminant hepatic failure
O bstetrical complications (eclampsia, preeclampsia, abruptio placenta, amniotic fluid embolus, retained placenta)
T umors: PML (AML, Type III, or "M3"); prostate carcinoma; mucin-secreting tumors of the pancreas[2]; breast ca; lymphoma
Tissue Trauma (burns, crush injuries, gunSHOT wounds), hemolytic Transfusion reactions (severe)
S urgery is the third leading cause; Snake venom

1. The mortality in DIC is often estimated around 50%, which is not much better than playing the S.L.O.T.S. ! 2. Mucin-producing cystic neoplasms of the pancreas account for 1% of all malignant tumors of the pancreas. They include mucinous cystic neoplasms (MCNs) and mucinous ductal ectasia (MDE), also known as intraductal mucin-hypersecreting neoplasms.

INDICATIONS FOR CHECKING SERUM DIGOXIN LEVEL: A.T. R.I.S.K.

A rrhythmias, newly-appearing
T

R efractory Afib
I nitiation of new treatment, esp. quinidine/amiodarone/spironolactone/verapamil.
S uspected toxicity
K idney—change in function

DIPTHERIA: D.I.P.T.H.E.R.I.A.

D iagnosis is established by culture or fluorescent Ab staining of pharyngeal swab specimen.

I nfection is caused by the gram positive, pleomorphic bacillus Corynebacterium diphtheriae.

P seudomembrane is the clinical hallmark of infection; the word 'diphtheria' derives from the Greek word for leather which refers to this tough pseudomembrane.

Prognosis & course of disease: the severity of disease is directly related to the time between the onset of symptoms and administration of antitoxin and to the severity of pharyngeal pseudomembrane formation and therefore toxin production; i.e. the more the pseudomembrane spreads from the tonsillopharyngeal area, the greater the systemic toxicity.

Polyneuritis → Neurologic toxicity is unusual in mild disease but develops in up to three-fourths of patients with severe diphtheria and can cause paralysis of the soft palate or posterior pharyngeal wall, followed by ocular/ciliary/facial/laryngeal cranial neuropathies and later peripheral neuritis, the most feared example of which is respiratory muscle paralysis.

T onsillopharyngeal involvement only in up to two-thirds of cases.

Toxin-mediated systemic complications: myocarditis & polyneuritis

H eart complications: myocarditis manifesting as ST-T wave changes and 1st degree AV block; but also advanced blocks, arrhythmias, CHF, and even circulatory collapse

E rythromycin or Pen; while neither alters the course of disease, they do prevent transmission to susceptible hosts. Close contacts should be evaluated and treated with Abx if culture results are +, and Td toxoid should be given.

R espiratory diphtheria is the most important clinical form of infection

I solate the patient. Patients with diphtheria need to be placed on respiratory droplet isolation for respiratory tract disease and contact isolation for cutaneous disease.

A ntitoxin-- The antitoxin is only effective before toxin enters the cell and thus must be administered early. Antitoxin is not commercially available in the United States, but may be obtained from the CDC

Antimicrobial Prophylaxis for close contacts — Close contacts need to be identified, cultured, and considered for antimicrobial prophylaxis. If immunizations are not up-to-date, they should also be given diphtheria-tetanus-pertussis or diphtheria-tetanus vaccine.

DLCO ↓: DIFFERENTIAL DIAGNOSIS: RE: PISA ↓
(as in "Remember: the leaning tower of Pisa is falling <u>down</u>")

R   ecurrent pulmonary emboli

E   mphysema

P   rimary Pulmonary HTN; <u>P</u>neumonectomy

I   diopathic Pulmonary Fibrosis

S   arcoidosis

A   nemia

DLCO ↑:   DIFFERENTIAL DIAGNOSIS ☞ "S.O.A.P. up ! "   <u>or</u>   S.H.A.P.E. up!

S   hunts, left-to-right

<u>S</u>upine posture

O   besity

A   lveolar hemorrhage, (Goodpasture's, Mitral Stenosis, Trauma);

<u>A</u>sthma

<u>A</u>fter exercise

P   olycythemia

or …

S   hunts, left-to-right

<u>S</u>upine posture

H   emorrhage, alveolar (Goodpasture's, Mitral Stenosis, Trauma);

<u>H</u>eavy patient (obesity)

A   sthma

P   olycythemia

E   xercise

✪ Current DMARD Therapies for RA:
"*GOLD PILE SCAM*"

DMARD	POTENTIAL TOXICITIES Requiring Monitoring	MONITORING STUDIES
Gold IM / PO	Myelosuppression, proteinuria	CBC and urine dipstick for protein, RFTs (Renal Function Tests)
Penicillamine	Myelosuppression, proteinuria	CBC and urine dipstick for protein
Infliximab (Remicade®) (IV)	Flu-like sx, auto-Abs; for patients not responding to methotrexate; URI; dyspnea; chest pain; sinusitis; hypotension	Baseline PPD, CXR, CBC; contraindicated in active infections
Leflunomide (Arava®)	Thrombocytopenia, hepatotoxicity, diarrhea; alopecia; HTN	CBC; AST; RFTs; Hep B & C testing
Etanercept (Enbrel®)	Reactions at site of SQ injection, flu-like sx; auto-Abs	Baseline PPD, CXR, CBC; contraindicated in active infections
Sulfasalazine	Myelosuppression, discoloration of urine/sweat/tears; leucopenia; reversible oligospermia; hepatitis	CBC, LFTs
Cyclophosphamide	Myelosuppression, myeloproliferative disorders, malignancy, hemorrhagic cystitis	CBC, urinalysis, and urine cytology
Cyclosporine	Renal insufficiency, anemia, HTN, hirsutism; gingival hyperplasia	Creatinine, CBC, K+, LFTs
Azathioprine	Myelosuppression, hepatotoxicity, lymphoproliferative disorders	CBC
Antimalarial: Hydroxychlorquine	Maculopathy	Yearly ophthalmologic exams
Adalimumab (Humira)	Sinusitis, URI, injx site pain, rash	Baseline PPD, CXR, CBC; contraindicated in active infections
Anakinra	URI, neutropenia, other infections	Baseline PPD, CXR, CBC; contraindicated in active infections
Methotrexate	Myelosuppression, hepatic fibrosis, cirrhosis, interstitial pneumonitis, pulmonary fibrosis	Baseline CXR, PFTs, LFTs, CBC, then periodic CBC, LFTs

DRUG-INDUCED PERIPHERAL NEUROPATHIES: DITCH MAP

D idanosine (ddI); ddC (zalcitabine); d4T (stavudine)
I soniazid
T axol
C isplatin (& vincristine)
H ydralazine

M etronidazole
A miodarone
P henytoin; Pyridoxine

PULMONARY INFILTRATES—DRUGS CAUSING: BN Gold CHAMP!

B leomycin, Busulfan, BCNU
N itrofurantoin

G old

C yclophosphamide, Chlorambucil
H ydralazine
A miodarone, Acyclovir, Azathioprine
M ethotrexate, Methylsergide, Melphalan, Mitomcyin
P enicillamine, Phenytoin, Paclitaxel, Procainamide

MEDS FREQUENTLY ASSOCIATED WITH ESOPHAGITIS

QUINcy PAID 'N Cash

Q uinidine

P otassium chloride
A lendronate/Aspirin
I ron sulfate
D oxycycline/Tetracycline

'N SAIDs

C vitamin

CYCLOSPORINE (CSA) LEVELS—IMPORTANT DRUGS THAT CAN ↑:

DECK (as in stacking the deck):

D iltiazem
E rythromycin
C imetidine
K etoconazole

DUKE'S CLASSIFICATION FOR COLORECTAL CA:

Stage	Definition	Treatment
A	Limited to mucosa/submucosa	Surgery
B1	Muscularis mucosa	Surgery
B2	*SEROSA* (into or through)	Surg + Chemo

(*Remember*, when it comes to the boards, one can never **B2 SERious**.)

Stage	Definition	Treatment
C1	+ regional lymph node mets ≤4	Surg + Chemo
C2	+ regional lymph node mets >4	Surg + Chemo
D	Distant mets	Surg + Chemo

DYSPHAGIA FOR SOLID <u>OR</u> LIQUID FOODS: SAD

S cleroderma
A chalasia
D iffuse Esophageal Spasm

DYSPHAGIA FOR SOLID FOODS ONLY: CRAP

C arcinoma of the esophagus
R ing (Schatski's)
A nd ...
P eptic stricture

ERYTHEMA NODOSUM: ASSOCIATED CONDITIONS: "Yer Leg BUMPS"

Y **er**sinia enterocolytica.

L öfgren's syndrome; Lymphoma

B ehcet's (defined as recurrent painful oral ulcers plus any 2 of the following: Ocular lesions; Skin lesions; Genital ulcers; and Pathergy test);

U lcerative Colitis (Crohn's too)

M TB; Mycoses

P arasites, Pregnancy, Pills (OCPs)

S ulphonamides, Strep pharyngitis, Sarcoidosis

ECTHYMA GANGRENOSUM: PAINLESS

P ainless & mildly tender (initially!)
Prolonged, profound neutropenia is often the clinical setting

A cutaneous manifestation of P aeruginosa sepsis (& other gram negatives); EG occurs in only 2% to 6% of patients with Pseudomonas sepsis. Mortality rates depend on the severity of the underlying sepsis.

I mmunocompromised patients; Initial manifestation (often) of systemic infection (bacteremia/sepsis).

N ecrotizing vasculitis of venules and arterioles without intimal damage. By contrast to cellulites, where the biopsy typically shows a marked inflammatory response and relatively few bacteria, in EG you see minimal inflammatory tissue reaction and high counts of bacteria.

L eukaemics, burns patients and the immunocompromised.

E schar: following a progression from Infection → infarction → hemorrhagic bullae/blisters/vesicles → ulcers with necrotic gangrenous bases → central, necrotic eschar with elevated hemorrhagic borders

S urgical debridement with subsequent graft coverage of the resultant tissue defect.+ IV Antibiotics.

S olitary (usually); may be multiple

HERE'S AN _EASIER WAY_ TO FIGURE THE AXIS: "RULE OF THUMBS" ™...

<u>Look at the direction of the R-wave in leads I and aVF:</u>

	I	aVF
Normal axis ("2 thumbs up")	↑	↑
LAD	↑	↓
RAD	↓	↑
Extreme RAD	↓	↓

ENCAPSULATED ORGANISMS: CAN SPIKE T !

C ryptococcus
A nthracis bacillus
N eisseria meningitidis

S treptococcus pneumoniae
P estis (yersinia)
I nfluenza (hemophilus)
K lebsiella
E Coli

T ularemia

INDICATIONS FOR EP STUDY: SCAR

S yncope, unexplained
C atheter ablation, evaluation for feasability
A ntiarrhythmic medications--determine response to
R ecurrent VT (also patients at high risk for VT); <u>R</u>ecurrent SVT of unknown mechanism

EOSINOPHILIA—DIFFERENTIAL: PANIC

P arasites

A llergy; Asthma

N eoplasms

I nsufficiency, adrenal

C ollagen vascular diseases

THE LOW-DOWN ON ERYTHEMAS: "E Gads!!"

E. *Nodosum*

E. *Chronicum Migrans* (ECM) → Lyme Disease

E. *Marginatum* → transient truncal rash in Rheumatic Fever

E. *Multiforme* → Stephen Johnson Syndrome (e.g.Dilantin, Sulfa, PCN, HSV, Mycoplasma)

E. *Gyratum Repens* (looks like the grain pattern of wood) → Internal malignancy (e.g. breast ca);

G lucagonoma → *Necrolytic Migratory* Erythema (NME)

ESOPHAGEAL SQUAMOUS CELL CA—RISK FACTORS #1: E.A.T. T.I.P.S.

E sophageal strictures, webs, rings, diverticuli

A lcohol; Achalasia

T ylosis

T obacco

I ngestion (smoked or pickled foods (nitrosamines); lye)

P lummer-Vinson Syndrome

S moking

ESOPHAGEAL SQUAMOUS CELL CA—RISK FACTORS #2:   A.S. S.P.E.L.T !*

A chalasia
S moking

S moked or pickled foods
P lummer-Vinson syndrome
E thanol abuse
L ye
T ylosis

* British, past of spell

EXTRAARTICULAR MANIFESTATIONS OF RA: MD Felt SPLEAN

M ononeuritis multiplex, Myocarditis
D igital infarction

F elty's syndrome

S jogren's syndrome
P leuritis, Pneumoconiosis (Caplan's syndrome), Pericarditis
L eukocytoclastic vasculitis, Low pleural fluid glucose, Leukocytosis, Lymphadenopathy
E yes: Episcleritis/uveitis
A nemia, Amyloidosis (spleen intentionally mispelt; think: "A" for RA)
N odules (skin and pulmonary)

EXTRAVASCULAR HEMOLYSIS: "H.E.M.A.T.ology *Extras*!"

H ypersplenism
E nzyme deficiency (G6PD deficiency)
M embrane disorders (hereditary spherocytosis, hereditary elliptocytosis)
A utoimmune hemolytic anemias (IgG warm auto-Ab (IgG); cold agglutinin disease (IgM, complement); PCH; drug-induced hemolysis)
T halassemia

INTRAVASCULAR HEMOLYSIS: MAPS

M **A**HA (Microangiopathic Hemolytic Anemia; fragmentation hemolysis)
  ➤ Direct trauma—repeated pounding hands or feet
  ➤ Damaged or prosthetic heart valve, severe DIC, certain medications, accelerated hypertension
  ➤ TTP/HUS (MAHA + thrombocytopenia + frank renal failure)
P NH—sucrose lysis and Ham's acid hemolysis tests
S ickle Cell Disease

FEATURES OF FACTOR XIII DEFICIENCY: FOUND Postop !

F FP in management
O pposite of factor XII deficiency in that Factor XII deficiency shows elevated coags--↑PTT—but no bleeding)
U rease clot solubility test is positive (special clot stability assay)
N ormal routine clotting tests (eg platelets, PT, PTT, bleeding time, thrombin time)
D elayed post-op bleeding (eg 24-26h after dental extraction)

P oor wound healing; clots are mechanically weak

FACTORS INVOLVED IN THE FINAL COMMON PATHWAY: "2 X 5 = 10"

Factors 10, 5, & 2 are shared by both the Extrinsic & Intrinsic Pathways. So, anything that affects one of these factors will increase PT *and* PTT.

A breakdown of the final steps of the coagulation cascade shows:

  ◆ Factor **10 + 5** take Prothrombin → Thrombin (Factor **2**), which in turn takes Fibrinogen → Fibrin. Then Factor 13 helps to cross-link the fibrin monomers.

FAMILIAL HYPOCALCIURIC HYPERCALCEMIA (FHH):   AMOR'S PUB

A utosomal dominant hypercalcemia in a relatively young patient
M ust be ruled out when diagnosing primary hyperparathyroidism PH)
O bviates parathyroidectomy!!
R esults in almost all cases from an inactivating mutation in the calcium-sensing receptor gene
S creening of family members is appropriate; surgical exploration is not!

P TH is ↔ to slightly ↑, and therefore, cannot be used to differentiate between PH and FFH
U rine Ca ↓ and is quite useful in differentiating PH & FHH. Urinary excretion of cyclic AMP is NORMAL, however, *versus* increased excretion in states of PTH excess.
B enign condition

FARMER'S LUNG: BET THE FARM

B ibasilar rales; <u>B</u>AL can show lymphocytosis* and antibody
E xposure to fungal antigens in moldy hay (especially) leads to fever/chills/sweats/dry cough/ dyspnea/headache/malaise 4-6 hours after exposure. The symptoms often last for 12 hours, and resolve spontaneously. This can occur again with each reexposure.
T wo phases: acute and subacute/chronic

T reatment: The acute phase tends to resolve spontaneously; the subacute/chronic phase may require treatment with prednisone
H ypersensitivity pneumonitis (another descriptor; farmer's lung is actually just an example of HP)
E osinophilia and wheezing are UNUSUAL; <u>E</u>SR ↑

F ungal precipitans (thermophilic actinomycetes) are the culprit allergens and are almost always positive in the serum
A voidance of exposure to antigen is the most important mgmt principle
R estrictive pattern is often noted with reduced lung volumes and decreased DLCO
M oldy hay is the biggest source of these fungal precipitans, but grain & silage are also common sources.

* The number of lymphocytes, particularly T cells, may be increased in hypersensitivity pneumonitis (as in sarcoidosis). However, whereas the CD4+ (helper/inducer) cells tend to predominate in active sarcoidosis, the CD8+ (suppressor/cytotoxic) T-cell subset may predominate in HP.

FELTY'S SYNDROME: FELT L.U.M.P.S.

L ymphadenopathy
U lcers on legs
M arrow effects: thrombocytopenia, hemolytic anemia. Infection may follow.
P igmentation of skin
S plenomegaly

DDX OF FEVER + PURPURA: MERSA*

M eningococcemia
E ndocarditis
R MSF
S epsis
∀ asculitis

    * Might also help you recall the endocarditis & sepsis; use ∀ as upside-down 'A'.

FIBROMYALGIA: KEY THERAPEUTIC OPTIONS: PABST !

P ain or rehabilitation clinic; Psychiatric support (as needed) for mood disturbances
A nalgesics (NSAIDs)
B enzodiazepines
S SRIs; Sleep center referral (prn)
T CAs; Trigger point injections

FIBROMYALGIA: SUMMARY OF KEY POINTS: **F.A.C.H.E.I.N.G.**

F   emale >> male; <u>F</u>atigue

A   bsence of inflammatory muscle or joint disease on exam

C   FS (<u>C</u>hronic Fatigue Syndrome)—big Crossover: close relationship
between the chronic fatigue syndrome and fibromyalgia. Not only are
diagnostic criteria for CFS similar to those for fibromyalgia, but the
majority of patients with CFS meet tender point criteria for
fibromyalgia; moreover, about 70 % of fibromyalgia patients meet
the criteria for CFS.

<u>C</u>entral Nervous System: It is also felt that the CNS may be
responsible for the abnormal pain perception in fibromyalgia. Sleep &
mood disturbances found in the majority of patients also seem to
support this theory.

H   eadaches

E   xam → look for tender or "trigger" points (≥ 11 for dx)

I   rritable Bowel Syndrome

N   o lab tests remarkable

G   eneralized, chronic pain

MEDICAL CONDITIONS THAT ↑ RISK FOR GASTRIC CANCER:

SAM's PUB!

S   urgery (prior gastric)

A   lcohol (!); <u>A</u>trophic gastritis (below) (*H. pylori* → chronic atrophic
gastritis→gastric ca)

M   enetrier's disease (extreme hypertrophy of the gastric rugal folds)

P   ernicious anemia

U   lcers (gastric)

B   lood type A

GIARDIASIS: IMPORTANT FEATURES: WARM FLOW

W   ater links: white <u>water</u> rafting trips/camping/hiking; well <u>water</u>; <u>watery</u> diarrhea (initially) <u>beginning suddenly about 1 week following exposure</u>; later foul-smelling, fatty stools (steatorrhea); <u>weeks</u> lasting: prolonged duration, often lasting at least 2-4 weeks

A   ntigen assays of the stool (ELISA or immunofluorescence) are useful in addition to O&P

R   outes of transmission: fecal-oral (person-to-person, food-borne, waterborne)

M   etronidazole

F   <u>latulence, bloating, cramping,</u>

L   eukocytosis/fecal Leukocytes usually NOT seen; neither is eosinophilia (an important exception for parasites)

O   &P (stool microscopy)

W   <u>eight loss</u> significant (≥10% in 50% of patients)

GLOMERULAR DISEASE WITH ↓ COMPLEMENT: Cold ALPINE

C   ryoglobulinemia ("Cold!")

A   bscess (visceral)

L   upus (SLE)

P   ost-streptococcal GN

I   diopathic membranoproliferative GN

N   ephritis

E   ndocarditis (subacute)

GLUCAGONOMA: SCAN WARDS

S tomatitis, glossitis
C holesterol low
A lpha cell pancreatic tumor $\rightarrow$ glucagon excess (>500 pg/mL)
N ormochromic normocytic anemia—felt most likely due to anemia of chronic disease

W eight loss
A bdominal CT is the initial imaging procedure of choice
R ash: Necrolytic migratory erythema
D iabetes mellitus; <u>D</u>iarrhea; <u>D</u>VT (thromboembolism)
S omatostatin for diarrhea (it's first-line therapy for symptomatic glucagonoma in patients with unresectable tumors); *anticoagulants* for any thromboses; *embolization* and chemoembolization of the hepatic artery in order to starve liver mets when somatostatin fails to control symptoms; insulin if required. <u>S</u>low-growing tumors (though usually advanced by the time of diagnosis). Even when mets are present, many patients experience prolonged survival with a combination of surgical debulking, somatostatin, and embolization.

CONDITIONS ASSOCIATED WITH GOUT: "That's a *HARD* 1 ! "

H TN
A therosclerosis
R enal stones
D M

COMMON CAUSES OF URIC ACID <u>UNDEREXCRETION</u>:   "That's *HARD* 2 !"

H TN
   Hyp<u>O</u>thyroidism
   Hyp<u>ER</u>parathyroidism
A cidosis (Lactic acidosis, DKA, starvation ketosis)
R enal insufficiency
D rugs (esp. thiazide diuretics; alcohol)

COMMON CAUSES OF <u>OVERPRODUCTION:</u>   *MORE HELP* for you guys !

M yeloproliferative diseases
O besity
R habdomyolysis
E thanol

H emolytic processes
E xercise
L ymphoproliferative diseases
P. Vera; <u>P</u>soriasis; <u>P</u>urine-rich diet

Other provocative factors include: stress, trauma, surgery, hospitalization, hyperalimentation, starvation, weight reduction, and infection.

GRAM POSITIVE RODS: LANCES

L isteria
A ctinomyces
N ocardia
C orynebacterium
E rysipelothrix
S treptomyces

GRAPEFRUIT JUICE: INTERACTING DRUGS: C. A. MISHAP or CLASH!
(*shared CYP3A4 metabolism*):

C alcium channel blockers (felodipine, nimodipine, nisolodipine, nitrendipine, pranidipine)

A miodarone

M ethadone
I mmunosuppressants (eg cyclosporine)
S ildenafil; <u>S</u>aquinavir (protease inhibitor)
H MG-CoA reductase inhibitors
A ntihistamines (ebastine, terfenadine)
P sychiatric meds (buspirone, carbamazepine, triazolam, midazolam, diazepam)
or ...

C affeine, <u>C</u>CBs, <u>C</u>arbamazepine, <u>C</u>lomipramine, <u>C</u>yclosporine
L osartan
A miodarone
S aquinavir, <u>S</u>ertraline, <u>S</u>ildenafil
H MG CoA reductase inhibitors (statins)

GYNECOMASTIA: KEY CAUSES: MAIDEN STOCK <u>**or**</u> DEMONIC TASK

M arijuana
A lcohol
I soniazid; <u>I</u>nhibition of testosterone
D igoxin
E strogen
N ormal adolescence

S pironolactone
T umors (Testicular and adrenal)
O ld age
C irrhosis; <u>C</u>imetidine; <u>C</u>alcium channel blockers
K etoconazole

or…

D igoxin
E strogen
M arijuana
O ld age
N ormal adolescence
I soniazid; <u>I</u>nhibition of testosterone
C irrhosis; <u>C</u>imetidine; <u>C</u>alcium channel blockers

T umors (Testicular and adrenal)
A lcohol
S pironolactone
K etoconazole

DRUGS THAT CAN LEAD TO GYNECOMASTIA: CDC's IM DEPT

C imetidine

D igoxin

C ytotoxic agents (via testicular damage)

S pironolactone

I soniazid

M ethyldopa

D iazepam

E strogens and androgens

P henothiazines

T ricyclic antidepressants

HAART (Highly Active AntiRetroviral Therapy)

- ✓ The *following* <u>combinations</u> *should be* **<u>avoided</u>** (2° to overlapping toxicity or reduced efficacy):

  - Stavudine (d**4**T) + **Z**DV → *remember*: 4Z (**4 z extra point**!)

  - dd**C** + dd**I** → *remember*: CI (as in the commonly used abbreviation for **C**ontra**I**ndicated)

  - **In**dinavir + **sa**quinavir → *remember*: **INSA**ne to use together

  - **3**TC + d**4**T → *remember*: "**3,4** out the door!"

HAPTOGLOBIN, HEMOSIDERIN, HEMOGLOBINURIA, HEMOSIDERINURIA:

Remember, after RBC lysis, the carrier protein **haptoglobin** binds Hgb; the hemoglobin-haptoglobin complex is rapidly removed by the liver, leading to a reduction in plasma haptoglobin. *If* the haptoglobin-binding capacity of the plasma is *exceeded*, free hemoglobin is left to pass through the glomeruli on its own. If this happens, the filtered hemoglobin is reabsorbed by the proximal tubule, where it is broken down, and the heme iron becomes incorporated into storage proteins (ferritin and **hemosiderin**). Staining the sediment with Prussian blue can help check for the presence of hemosiderin in the urine. A positive stain indicates that a significant amount of circulating free hemoglobin has been filtered by the kidneys. Hemosiderin usually appears 3 to 4 days after the onset of hemoglobinuria. So, in summary, there's **Lysis → Hgb-Haptoglobin complex → Hgburia → Hemosiderinuria.**

HEMOCHROMATOSIS—IMPORTANT COMPLICATIONS: **I. A.C.H.E. !**

I   ntegument—skin bronzing ("bronze diabetes")

A   rthropathy (Aches!)
C   ardiac (CHF, arrhythmias)
H   epatic (hepatomegaly; cirrhosis → hepatocellular carcinoma)
E   ndocrine (diabetes, hypogonadism {impotence, ↓libido, amenorrhea}, hypopituitarism)

HEMOCHROMATOSIS—*IRREVERSIBLE* COMPLICATIONS: **H.A.G.**

H   epatic (cirrhosis; carcinoma)
A   rthropathy
G   onads (hypogonadism)

HEMOLYSIS DUE TO CELLULAR DEFECTS: **SHIP**

S   hape abnormalities: spherocytes, elliptocytes ovalocytes)
H   emoglobinopathies: SS anemia, thalassemia
I   ntrinsic enzyme defects
P   NH

LABS IN HEMOLYTIC ANEMIA: CRUSH Labs

C oomb's test (+ in direct; - in indirect)

R eticulocytosis

U nconjugated bili ↑; Urine hemosiderin[1] test +; Urine Hgb[1] +

S chisocytes; ± Spherocytes; ± Sickle cells

H aptoglobin[1] ↓

L DH ↑

[1] *Intravascular* Hemolysis:

1. **H**emoglobinemia

2. **H**emoglobinuria

3. **M**ethemoglobinemia

4. **H**emosidinuria

5. **H**aptoglobin (serum) ↓

OVERVIEW OF HEMOLYTIC DISORDERS

CONGENITAL CONDITIONS: H.E.Me.

H emoglobinopathies:
- Homozygous sickle cell disease (hemoglobin SS disease)
- Heterozygous sickle hemoglobin C disease (hemoglobin SC disease)

E nzyme deficiencies (RBC) :
- Glucose-6-phosphate dehydrogenase deficiency
- Pyruvate kinase deficiency

M embranes Disorders (RBC) :
- Hereditary spherocytosis
- Hereditary elliptocytosis

ACQUIRED CONDITIONS: *"Acquired a* **M.A.P.**"

M echanical hemolysis

- Macrovascular disorders (mechanical valves, etc)
- Microangiopathic disorders (MAHA=microangiopathic hemolytic anemia): eg DIC; HUS/TTP

A utoimmune hemolytic anemias

- Warm-reactive anemias
- Cold-reactive anemias
- Drug-induced anemias

P aroxysmal nocturnal hemoglobinuria (PNH)

HEMOLYTIC ANEMIAS: **SHEER IT**

S ickle cell anemia

H ereditary spherocytosis; Hemoglobinuria, Paroxysmal Nocturnal (PNH)

E nzyme deficiencies: eg G6PD; pyruvate kinase

E rythroblastosis fetalis

R BC trauma

I mmunohemolytics: warm and cold Ab

T halassemias

HEMOPTYSIS—MOST COMMON CAUSES: **B.L.T.**

B ronchiectasis; Bronchitis

L ung carcinoma

T B

HENOCH-SCHÖNLEIN PURPURA: PAINS <u>or</u> GAP USA

P alpable purpura (most commonly distributed over the buttocks and lower extremities)

A thritis/arthralgias, <u>A</u>bdominal PAINS

I g A is the culprit in this immune-complex disease; IgA levels are in fact ↑ in half the patients; <u>I</u>nfection of the upper respiratory tract a common precipitant {not unlike Berger's (Ig A nephropathy!) and poststreptococcal GN (and Guillain Barre for that matter)}

N ephritis

S mall vessel vasculitis; <u>S</u>pontaneous resolution of disease or improvement with <u>S</u>teroids is the usual course

or …

G astrointestinal signs and symptoms, and <u>G</u>lomerulonephritis.

A rthralgias

P alpable purpura (most commonly distributed over the buttocks and lower extremities)

U RI—common precipitant {not unlike Berger's (Ig A nephropathy!) and poststreptococcal GN}

S mall vessel vasculitis; <u>S</u>pontaneous resolution of disease or improvement with <u>S</u>teroids is the usual course

A (Ig A) is the culprit antibody in this immune-complex disease, and in fact, IgA levels are elevated in about one-half of patients.

HEPATIC VEIN THROMBOSIS MAY COMPLICATE THESE: HOPING
(as in "hoping" you remember these !)

H epatoma

O CPs—as noted above

P Vera; <u>P</u>NH

I BD

N ephro**G**enic carcinoma (renal cell ca)

HEPATITIS B—KEY CLINICAL ASSOCIATIONS TO KNOW: "B A CHAMP!"

A plastic Anemia

C ryoglobulinemia, mixed (Hep C > B)
H epatocellular carcinoma
A rthralgias
M embranous (MGN) and Membranoproliferative glomerulonephritis
(MPGN) are the most common assoc'd GNs
P AN

HEPATITIS C—KEY CLINICAL ASSOCIATIONS TO KNOW:

"C. Mi Pita Me.L.T.S." or, (if you want a drink with that order)…"C. S.P.iL.T. M.ilk"

M ixed Cryoglobulinemia (Hep C > B)

P orphyria cutanea tarda; Plasmacytoma

M embranoproliferative GN
L eukocytoclastic vasculitis; Lichen Planus; Lymphoma (B cell)
T hyroiditis
S jogren's Syndrome

or …

S jogren's Syndrome
P orphyria cutanea tarda; Plasmacytoma
L eukocytoclastic vasculitis; Lichen Planus; Lymphoma (B cell)
T hyroiditis

M ixed cryoglobulinemia (Hep C > B)

✪ **THE 'RULE OF 20s' WITH HEP C:**

> ➤ **20%** of patients with acute Hep C have *symptoms*
> ➤ 15-**20%** of patients with acute Hep C *clear the virus*
> ➤ In **20%** to 40% of patients with chronic Hep C, *cirrhosis* develops over **20** years
> ➤ Cirrhosis leads to *liver failure* in **20%** of these patients, and to *HCC* in another **20%**
> ➤ **20%** of patients without cirrhosis who receive *interferon* will obtain a *sustained response*.

HEPATOMEGALY + HEART FAILURE—NOT JUST CHF: CHA CHA

C onstrictive pericarditis
H eart Failure—left or right
A lcoholic cardiomyopathy with fatty liver

C arcinoid syndrome
H emochromatosis
A myloidosis

HEPATORENAL SYNDROME: FACT DUMP!

F ailure to respond to a fluid challenge can help distinguish HRS from hypovolemia (prerenal indices can look similar)

A RF with normal tubular function/normal urinalysis/benign sediment in a patient with cirrhosis or less often liver mets or severe alcoholic hepatitis

C reatinine concentration above 1.5 mg/dL (133 µmol/L) that progresses over days to weeks in patients with severe acute or chronic liver disease with portal hypertension.

T reatment is largely supportive. Patients with hepatorenal syndrome who progress to renal failure can be treated with dialysis. Survival on dialysis is generally limited by the severity of the hepatic failure. The best hope for reversal of the renal failure is an improvement in hepatic function due to partial resolution of the primary disease or to successful hepatic transplantation.

D iagnosis of exclusion, ie requires the absence of any other apparent cause for the renal disease

U rine sodium is < 10 meq/L (off diuretics) and urine osm > plasma osm.

M ortality is high. Distinguishing HRS from other disorders is important clinically because of the marked difference in prognosis. Acute tubular necrosis, for example, and other causes of prerenal disease are generally reversible.

P recipitated by: acute insult such as gastrointestinal bleeding, infection, or aggressive diuresis, all of which are common scenarios in cirrhosis.

HEREDITARY HEMORRHAGIC TELANGIECTASIA: F.A.T.A.L. O.N.E.
(OSLER-WEBER-RENDU SYNDROME)

F amily history

A utosomal dominant

T elangiectasias: lips (classic), face, nares, tongue, ears, hands, chest and feet

A VMs → esp GI (bleeds) and pulmonary (hemoptysis)

L ongevity is *not* inevitably reduced nor is the quality of life necessarily impaired; nonetheless, bleeds can be 'fatal ones'!

O blood type occurs with relatively greater frequency in these individuals.

N eurologic complications in 8-12%; peak incidence in the third to fourth decades. They usually result from (1) pulmonary A-V fistula, (2) vascular malformation of the brain (28%) and spinal cord (8%), and (3) portosystemic encephalopathy (3%). It is important to remember that asymptomatic pulmonary arteriovenous fistula may present initially as cerebral embolism (paradoxical embolism since bypasses the pulmonary capillary filter) or brain abscess.

E pistaxis, recurrent

HEREDITARY ANGIONEUROTIC EDEMA (HANE):   F.A.T. L.I.P.S.

F amily history and a marked increase in attacks at adolescence is highly suggestive of this inherited form. However, in more than 20% of those with hereditary angioedema, the mutations are de novo and therefore there is *no* family history of the disease.

A ngioedema is recurrent, painless, nonpruritic, nonerythematous. There is NO urticaria in angioedema due to C1 INH deficiency. Adolescence: onset of attacks, which continue throughout life.

T erminology: C1 INH, or C1 inhibitor deficiency is also called C1 *esterase* inhibitor, but the shorter name is better, because the esterase only refers to something which happens in lab tests, not in the body. Hereditary angioedema (HAE) used to be called 'hereditary angioneurotic edema' (HANE), but there is no evidence it has anything to do with nerves.

L ips (hallmark sign)/eyes/penis*:* affects mucocutaneous junctions*.* Glottal edema may complicate, esp if angioedema occurs in the context of anaphylaxis. Occasional GI tract involvement can mimic acute abdominal syndromes but without associated with fever, peritoneal signs, or an elevated white blood cell count and resolves spontaneously in 48 to 72 hours, and can lead to unnccessary laparotomy.

I NH deficiency, C1 (C1 inhibitor INH deficiency), whose function is preventing unnecessary activation of the complement system; therefore C1 is *disinhibited*, and thus the symptoms); C4 levels are usually also ↓. Among HANE families, approx 20% have *functionally defective* C1 esterase inhibitor (HANE type II). In approx 80%, both levels and functional activity of C1 esterase inhibitor were low (HANE type I).

P recipitants: trauma (mild) and anxiety are very common precipitants of hereditary angioedema.

S tanozolol danazol (attenuated androgens) may be useful as both acute and prophylactic therapy by increasing the plasma concentrations of C1-INH (via enhanced hepatic synthesis) and C4. Treatment of the acute episode is with FFP.

IMPORTANT DERMATOLOGIC INFECTIONS COMMON IN HIV: **C. Z.O.M.B.I.E.S.**

C ondyloma acuminata: genital, anorectal warts; Cervical or anorectal dysplasia and Carcinoma → HPV

Z oster/VZV

O ral hairy leukoplakia →EBV and usually seen in advanced AIDS. Treatment is acyclovir / antivirals (*Note*: this is *not* the same as "oral leukoplakia", which is related to HPV, smoking, smokeless tobacco, alcohol, and syphilis. Candida can invade oral leukoplakia secondarily, and it is considered a premalignant lesion for squamous cell ca)

M olluscum contagiosum (Poxvirus)→ Discrete, solid, skin-colored papules that are only 1-2 mm in diameter, have central umbilication

B acillary angiomatosis (vascular papules or nodules caused by Bartonella (Rochalimaea) henselae and quintana and transmitted by cats or ticks) → Erythromycins or Doxycycline for treatment

I ntertrigenous candida albicans

E xanthem of acute HIV itself (present in up to 50% of patients with acute HIV syndrome and usually resolves spontaneously within 1-2 weeks; nonpruritic rash primarily over upper trunk, proximal limbs)

S arcoma, Kaposi's (HHV-8)
Seborrheic dermatitis (Pityrosporum ovale plays an important role)
Simplex, Herpes (HSV I, II)
Syphilis (Treponema pallidum: chancre, diffuse maculopapular rash
Staph aureas infections: most common cause of bacterial skin infections in HIV disease; folliculitis, bullous impetigo, ecthyma

INFECTIOUS CAUSES OF GI DISEASE IN HIV: **CHIC MAG** *(slang for "chick magnet")*

C ryptosporidium—Voluminous, watery diarrhea. In immunocompromised hosts, especially those with AIDS, diarrhea can be chronic, persistent, and remarkably profuse, causing clinically significant fluid and electrolyte depletion. Stool volumes may range from 1 to 25 L/d.no therapy proven efficacious, although in AIDS patients may try treating with paromomycin.; CMV (remember, in CMV infection, viremia does not necessarily correlate with organ involvment; therefore, cultures are often of no use in this setting); Candida esophagitis

H istoplasma capsulatum—colonic involvement; diagnosis by culture; treatment is ampho or itraconazole; HSV; remember also: when see Hairy Leukoplakia → must R/O HIV; Hominis (blastocystis hominis) → role as a pathogen is controversial; no controlled rx trials

I sospora belli- Diagnosis via oval oocysts in the stool seen with modified Kinyoun acid-fast stain. Primary treatment choice is TMP-SMX (160/800 mg qid for 10 days and then bid for 3 weeks) for treatment.

C yclospora--Some patients may harbor the infection without symptoms, but many with cyclosporiasis have diarrhea, flulike symptoms, and flatulence and burping. The diagnosis can be made by detection of spherical 8- to 10-um oocysts in the stool. These refractile oocysts are variably acid-fast and are fluorescent when viewed with ultraviolet light microscopy.

M AI (mycobacterium avium intracellulare) can cause a voluminous diarrhea and is often associated with additional fever, abdominal pain, and weight loss. Microsporidia— Affects the small intestine, causing diarrhea; albendazole is the primary treatment of choice.

A mebiasis (Entameba histolytica) → Metronidazole

G iardia lamblia ☞ Prominent early symptoms include watery diarrhea starting suddenly 1 week after exposure,cramping/bloating/ flatulence, significant weight loss. It frequently lasts several weeks. Transmission is fecal-oral. Giardia is associated with camping trips, white-water rafting, well-water; treatment is metronidazole

HLA-DR- ASSOCIATED CONDITIONS: DR. MALIGNANT

D iabetes, Type I
R heumatoid Arthritis

M yasthenia Gravis; <u>M</u>ultiple Sclerosis
A nemia, pernicious
L upus (systemic & drug-induced, eg hydralazine); <u>L</u>eukemia
I gA nephropathy (Berger's nephopathy); <u>I</u>gA deficiency
G oodpasture's disease; <u>G</u>raves' disease
N arcolepsy
A ddison's disease
N ephropathy, membranous
T hyroiditis; <u>T</u>hyroid ↑ or ↓

KEY FEATURES OF HPOA (Hypertrophic Pulmonary Osteoarthropathy):

PRICE/LB

P eriosteal new bone formation occurs at the end of long bones, giving tenderness and soft-tissue swelling → <u>P</u>ain on <u>P</u>alpation of the involved area and renders a so-called "spongy" sensation on palpation of the fingernail beds.
R emoval of lung cancer or treatment of the other causes of HOA results in regression in the clinical manifestations
I mproved pain on lowering the legs is characteristic when lower extremities are involved
C lubbing
E ndocarditis, bacterial, an important cause; <u>E</u>ffusions (synovial)

/

L ung carcinoma (primary or secondary) the other important etiology
B one scan ideal

HYPERCALCEMIA—CAUSES: MD SET HIP

M alignancy, <u>M</u>ilk-alkali syndrome
D ialysis/renal failure

S arcoidosis
E ndocrine disorders (Addison's, pheo, thyrotoxicosis)
T hiazide diuretics

H yperparathyroidism; <u>H</u>ypervitaminosis A & D
I mmobilization, <u>I</u>diopathic
P aget's disease

KNOW THESE IMPORTANT CAUSES OF ↑K+:   RHABDO

R habdomyolysis
H emolysis
A ddison's Disease
B ad kidneys (ARF, CRF)
D rugs (ACE I, K+ sparing diuretics)
O (hyp<u>o</u>renin hyp<u>o</u>aldo)

KNOW THE DDX FOR ↓ MG: ABCDEFGH

A TN, ↑ Aldo
B artter Syndrome
C yclosporin*, <u>C</u>isplatinum*
D iuretics
E thanol
F at losses (malabsorption syndromes)
G astric losses (NG suction, vomiting)
H ypoparathyroidism

CAUSES OF HYPERPROLACTINEMIA: "DAPHNE'S PEACHES" …

MEDICATIONS WHICH CAN INDUCE HYPERPROLACTINEMIA: DAPHNI'S

D opamine antagonists (eg metoclopramide)

A ntihypertensives (eg methyldopa, atenolol, reserpine, verapamil)

P sychotropics (most all classes: eg benzos, SSRI, TCA, MAOI, phenothiazines, etc)

H 2 Blockers; Hormonal preparations (oral contraceptives, medroxyprogesterone acetate, estrogen, danazol)

N eurologic medications:

  Sumatriptan (Imitrex)

  Valproic Acid (Depakene)

  Dihydroergotamine (DHE 45)

  Narcotics

I soniazid

  Illicit Drugs (MAO: marijuana; amphetamines; opiates)

S andostatin (octreotide)

GENERAL CAUSES OF HYPERPROLACTINEMIA: PEACHES

P hysiologic: pregnancy, nipple stimulation, exercise, intercourse, ill-fitting bras, etc)

E motional stress

A ll of the drugs listed above

C hest wall: injury; mass; herpes zoster

  CRF

H epatic cirrhosis

E ndocrine: prolactinomas; PCO; hypothyroidism; adrenal adenoma/tumor; ovarian tumor

S ynthesis inhibition of PIF (Prolactin Inhibitor Factor) from any number of causes directly affecting the hypothalamic: masses, infarctions, infiltrations, etc.; any process interrupting the pituitary stalk, and therefore the transport of PIF.

REMEMBER, <u>JUST AS HYPER</u>para <u>can be</u> 1°, 2°, and 3°, <u>so HYPO</u> para <u>can be</u>…

    a) **HYPOPARA-- ↓ PTH**

    b) **"PSEUDO" hypopara**—↑**PTH** (r/o ↓ vit D and renal failure); genetic; 2° to **end-organ resistance to PTH; urinary cAMP is** ↓

        Clinical—may see…

            (i)   Short stature/short neck/short metacarpals

            (ii)   Rounded face/obesity/mild mental retardation

            (iii) SQ Calcification

    c) **"PSEUDOPSEUDO"** hypopara—same as (b) **but without the biochemical markers**

ECHOCARDIOGRAPHIC FINDINGS CHARACTERISTIC OF IHSS:

SAM ASH

➢ **S**ystolic **A**nterior **M**otion of the anterior MV leaflet *with*

➢ **A**symmetric **S**eptal **H**ypertrophy"

INDICATIONS FOR IABP (Intra-Aortic Balloon Pump):   **IABP'S**

I schemia-related VTach

A ngina, unstable & refractory

B lood flow inadequate to sustain the organs due to cardiogenic shock

P apillary Muscle Rupture

S eptal defect, ventricular

IDIOPATHIC INTRACRANIAL HTN (IIH): **PSEUDO HINTS**

P SEUDOtumor Cerebri and Benign Intracranial HTN (the term "benign' is misleading really since a significant number go onto develop some degree of visual loss) are synonyms

S ystemic diseases associated include: HTN, sarcoidosis, lupus and ulcerative colitis

E ndocrine risk factors: **ACHE FROM** …

    A drenal insufficiency

    C ushing disease

    H ypothyroidism; Hypoparathyroidism

    E xcessive thyroxine replacement in children (ie, low TSH levels)

    but the most important ones are…

    F emale gender

    R eproductive age group

    O besity; recent weight gain

    M enstrual irregularity

U nknown cause

D rugs associated include: **TOAST**: **T**CN, **O**ral contraceptives, hypervitaminosis **A**, **S**teroids (corticosteroids), and **T**hyroxine replacement

O ptic atrophy and visual complaints in approximately 85% of patients common secondary to chronic papilledema. These may include transient episodes of blurred vision, diplopia, photosensitivity, photopsia, and scotomata. Visual disturbances are generally preceded by headache. Vision loss is the only serious long-term complication of IIH.

H eadache and papilledema (though papilledema is not necessary to make the diagnosis) in an obese women of childbearing age is the usual presentation

I ncreased intracranial pressure on LP (>200 mm water in the nonobese and >250 mm water in the obese patient); no intracranial mass

N ormal neuroimaging (CT or MRI)

T reatment options include: weight reduction, diuretics (acetazolamide), oral corticosteroids, occasionally a shunt, and optic nerve decompression

S ixth nerve palsy (CN VI, abducens)-- the best-recognized nonlocalizing neurological sign.

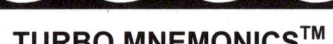

IMPORTANT CAUSES OF ↑ ACE LEVELS: A.C.E. T.R.A.M.P.S.

A ctive sarcoidosis
C hronic pulmonary disease
E ndocrine causes (Diabetes mellitus, HyperParathyroidism, HyperThyroidism)

T B, miliary
R heumatoid arthritis
A sbestosis
M ycoses (eg histoplasmosis)
P BC (Primary Biliary Cirrhosis)
S ilicosis

INDICATIONS FOR SURGERY IN INFECTIVE ENDOCARDITIS: SHAVE PAP !

S eptic emboli, repeated
H emolysis
A I, with refractory CHF
V egetations, large
E xtensive valve ring infection

P rosthetic valve involvement
A bscess-associated conduction disturbances
P ersistent bacteremias/fever despite optimal medical mgmt

LIVER DYSFUNCTION IN IBD: CCCHHH

C holelithiasis in Crohn's disease (re: "stones in Crohn's")
C holangiocarcinoma
C holangitis (either pericholangitis—usually minimally symptomatic ↑alk phos—or *sclerosing cholangitis*)

H epatitis (CAH)→cirrhosis; granulomatous)
H epatic infiltration (fat, amyloid)
H epatic vein thrombosis (*see next section*)

EXTRAINTESTINAL FEATURES OF IBD: **E. PEARLS !**

E ye conditions (conjunctivitis; uveitis; episcleritis)

P yoderma gangrenosum

E nodosum

A nkylosing spondylitis; <u>A</u>phthous ulcers; <u>A</u>rthropathy (transient; large joints)

R enal—oxalate stones

L iver disease

S acroiliitis

➢ This **PERIPHERAL** **arthritis** of IBD tends to occur ≥ 6 months after the onset of bowel disease. Its **severity reflects/Parallels that of the bowel disease**. Colectomy rids it.

➢ **Spondylitis/Sacroiliitis** (considered more **CENTRAL** arthritis) occur in ~ 5%, may predate the onset of bowel symptoms, and are **associated with HLA-B27**. They are **independent of bowel disease activity (or STAY the SAME)**, and so unaffected by colectomy.

➢ **So!** Peripheral **P**arallels disease; **S**pondyloarthropathy (more '**S**'entral disease of the axial skeleton; eg spondylitis/sacroiliitis) **S**tays the **S**ame.

➢ Among the extraintestinal manifestations: ***the severity of joint and skin disease mirrors the severity of colitis*** . On the other hand, ankylosing spondylitis and sacroiliitis do not mirror the colitis.

INTERVENTIONS THAT HAVE BEEN SHOWN TO ↓ MORTALITY AFTER MI:

"Take A STAB at it"

A SA should be administered at a dose of 160 to 325 mg ASAP after onset of symptoms and continued at ≥75 mg/day indefinitely thereafter. Ticlopidine and clopidogrel are alternative anti-platelet options. Clopidogrel is generally preferred because of fewer side effects.

S tatin therapy initiated prior to discharge reduces 1-year mortality by 34% and reduce the risk of a recurrent MI up to 40% even in patients with average cholesterol levels.

T hrombolytics/angioplasty

A CE Inhibitor 3 days out (only those with evidence of CHF or low EF% (≤ 40%) or cardiomegaly should remain on the ACEI)—these work to prevent so-called "remodeling" which can have an ill-effect following an MI.

B eta-blockers→beware in those with severe asthma. Beta-blockers work by decreasing the myocardial wall stress and the cardiac work load. Remember to follow the PR interval (<.24), the HR (>45), the SBP (>100), and check for rales before each dose of IV Beta-blockade. (a 5-5-5mg IV metoprololol at >2 min intervals is commonly used). MI patients should be continued on Beta-blockers, advancing to 50mg PO q6h x1 day, and then to 100mg PO bid indefinitely as tolerated.

Note: While *Nitrates* relieve pain, i.e. ↓ morbidity, they *do not ↓ mortality.* Don't be fooled.

INVASIVE BACTERIAL DIARRHEAS (Bloody stools; + fecal leukocytes; fever generally):

"Yer V.I.C.E.S.!"

Y ersinia enterocolitica

V ibrio vulnificus

I nvasive E. Coli (enteroinvasive E. Coli)

C ampylobacter jejuni; C diff. colitis (5% of cases present this way)

E Coli 0157H7

S almonella, Shigella

DIFFERENTIAL DIAGNOSIS OF AN IRREGULARLY IRREGULAR PULSE:

You look for Afib, but you might just get … S.P.A.M.

S inus arrhythmia

P VCs

A Fib; A Tach or A Flutter with variable block

M AT or WAP (wandering atrial pacemaker)

IRRITABLE BOWEL SYNDROME—KEY FEATURES: IBS DIAPER

I ncomplete evacuation, sense of

B owel movements ↑ in relation to stress

S leep--pain in IBS does not awaken the patient from sleep; <u>S</u>erotonin

modulators (eg 5-HT3, and 5-HT4) are important emerging

therapeutic tools

D iarrhea ± constipation; <u>D</u>istension; <u>D</u>yspepsia

I ncreased frequency of stools (defined by the Rome II criteria as: > 3

BMs/day <u>or</u> < 3 BMs/week)

A bdominal pain

P encil-thin stools

E nhanced visceral perception (eg to distension) in diarrhea-

predominant and pain-predominant IBS

R elieved by defecation

ISCHEMIC COLITIS: WASTING

W eight loss ("Wasting")

A bdominal pain: mild-to-moderate; Abdominal tenderness: minimal-to-moderate

S ubacute disease, producing less pain and bleeding and often occurring over several days or weeks.

Surgery is not required except for obstruction secondary to postischemic stricture;

Spontaneous resolution in most cases.

Satiety, early

T humbprinting here too.

I ndications: angiography NOT valuable as almost all cases are nonocclusive. Mucosal ischemia is a result of transient low blood flow or poor perfusion through atherosclerotic splanchnic vasculature as well as "watershed" area of the intestine

N /V /Diarrhea; nonocclusive in most cases

G I bleeding (lower GIB)

KARTAGENER'S SYNDROME (Immotile Cilia Syndrome): ICS

I nfertility common in males

C learance of bacteria is poor→ leading to infections of sinuses and bronchi

S itus inversus (i.e. dextrocardia) in 50%

- Note: The infertility in Kartagener's syndrome is 2° to immotility of the sperm, whereas in CF, it is 2° to azospermia (reflecting obliteration of the vas deferens)

KAWASAKI DISEASE: CECIL'S FAV

C onjunctivitis; Children predominantly

E rythematous rash to palms/soles

C ardiovascular sequelae: Coronary aneurysms classic

I diopathic generalized polymorphic rash

L ymphadenopathy (cervical)

S alicylate (ASA) important in management

F ever > 5 days

A neurysms, coronary

V asculitis, arterial

KAWASAKI'S DISEASE: CLINICAL MANIFESTATIONS: C FEVERS

C oronary artery aneurysms-- occur in 20-25% of children with the disease; generally occur within 3 to 6 months of the onset of the acute illness

F ever, prolonged (> 5 days)

E rythema (palms/soles); exfoliation (desquamation)
Edema of the dorsum of the hands

V asculitis, systemic, affecting small- and medium-sized arteries
Vertically cracked, or "fissured" lips

E yes: conjunctivitis that is bilateral & nonexudative; brilliant erythema which spares the limbus; anterior uveitis; photophobia

R heumatic: arthritis in 1/3 of children;
Rash: polymorphous skin eruption on the trunk

S trawberry tongue (erythematous tongue with prominent papillations; also seen in scarlet fever and toxic shock syndrome)
Swollen cervical lymph nodes—absent in as many as half the cases

KLINEFELTER'S SYNDROME: **BIG SHAME**

B one density ↓; <u>B</u>uccal smear (for karyotyping)

I ncreased height

G ynecomastia (incidentally, unilateral gynecomastia should
make one think of carcinoma);<u>G</u>erm cell tumors of the testes ↑
(risk factor for testicular ca)

S mall, firm testes; <u>S</u>HBG ↑ may result in normal-range testosterone
levels in approx. 40%

H ypergonadotropic hypogonadism (testosterone ↓; LH, FSH ↑)

A zospermia; infertility; <u>A</u>utoimmune disorders may be associated

M ental retardation, mild

E unuchoid habitus; <u>E</u>xtra X chromosome (47XXY karyotype)

✓ **Criteria for LAE**: Width > **3 boxes** (.12 s) or notched P wave in the inferior
leads or V1, V2; a biphasic P wave in V1 should also make you think of LAE.

✓ **Criteria for RAE**: Height > **2.5 boxes** (0.25 mV; 2 ½ small boxes), esp in
lead II

So remember, **"LEFT → LENGTH; RIGHT → HEIGHT"**

LETHARGY/MALAISE—CAUSES: **LUNAR TIDE**

L iver disease

U remia

N utrition poor

A nemia

R heumatic disorders (eg PMR)

T umor

I nfection

D epression; <u>D</u>iabetes; <u>D</u>rugs

E ndocrine (eg hypothyroidism; Addison's)

LEGIONNAIRES' DISEASE: "Lung, Liver, Lytes, Loose BMs"

L ung → **Bilateral patchy infiltrates; relatively nonproductive cough;** Patients with community-acquired Legionnaires' disease are much more likely than patients with pneumonia from other causes to be admitted to the ICU upon presentation.

L iver → **LFTs increase**

L ytes → **HYPONATREMIA**, hypophosphatemia

L oose BMs → **Diarrhea**

FEATURES DIFFERENTIATING LEUKEMOID REACTION* (from CML):

Not CML !

N onpalpable spleen

C hromosome (Philadelphia) absent

M yeloid elements: Mature polymorphs predominate (suppressed in CML) and Myeloblasts are unusual (can be > 80% in CML)

L AP (leukocyte alkalkine phosphatase) is ↑ (↓ as in CML)

*   Essentially a reactive leukocytosis in excess of 50,000/µL and entirely unrelated to leukemia with a marked "left shift," as evidenced by the presence of myelocytes and metamyelocytes, and increased numbers of band forms in the peripheral blood.

LITHIUM--SIDE EFFECTS: **LITHIUM**

L   eukocytosis; Loose BMs

I   ncreased weight; Irregular heartbeat; Impaired coordination

T   remor (fine); Teratogenesis

H   ypothyroidism

I   nsipidus (DI)

U   nsteady gait

M   uscle weakness; Memory impairment

CAUSES OF LOW-VOLTAGE EKG: ECG LOST

E ffusion, pericardial

C ardiomyopathy / myocarditis

G lobal ischemia

L ead placement (eg over breast tissue)

O besity

S tandardization off / calibration off

T amponade

LOWER LOBE INFILTRATES—IMPORTANT CAUSES: B HAPPI

B ronchiectasis

H ypersensitivity pneumonitis

A sbestosis

P ulmonary hemosiderosis

P ulmonary fibrosis

I diopathic Pulmonary Fibrosis (IPF)

Common Differential of Lupus Anticoagulant: Drug-using L.I.A.R.

D rugs (phenytoin, hydralazine, quinidine, procainamide)

L upus (SLE)

I TP

A IDS

R A

PARANEOPLASTIC ASSOCIATIONS IN LUNG CA:

✪ Remember, **S**MALL cell and **S**QUAMOUS cell ca lung ca are **Sentral** (centrally located).

✪ Remember too, just as **LARGE** cell and **ADENO** ca are peripheral, so either can result in "*peripheral*" findings as seen at the finger tips! (Hypertrophic Osteoarthopathy, HOA)

✪ SMALL CELL ☞ "CASES"

    C arcinoid
    A CTH ↑ (Cushing's syndrome)
    S IADH
    E aton-Lambert Syndrome (muscle weakness, noted in simple tasks like combing one's hair or rising from a chair; improves with effort/repetitive action
    S VC

> ☞ Remember the commonly quoted fact in small cell: "The #1 cause of death in survivors of small cell lung ca is *non-small* cell lung ca!" (from the chemo)

✪ **LARGE** CELL only → **gynecomastia** {this is a no-brainer}

LUNG CARCINOMA—NOTORIOUS COMPLICATIONS: "Gee S.H.A.P.E.S."
(as in what a radiology student might say on seeing his first CXR)

    G ynecomastia (large cell)

    S IADH (small cell), Spinal cord compression (mets), Subacute cerebellar degeneration (paraneoplastic)
    H orner's syndrome (squamous usually), Hoarseness, HPOA (large cell & adeno), Hypercalcemia (squamous cell)
    A CTH, ectopic (small cell) → Cushing's syndrome
    P ancoast's tumor, Pericardial tamponade (from lung mets)
    E aton-Lambert Syndrome
    S VC syndrome (small cell usually)

STAGING IN LUNG CARCINOMA

NON-SMALL CELL LUNG CA ✪

Stage	Criteria	Treatment
I	- Hilar nodes	**SURGERY**
II	+ Hilar nodes	**SURGERY**
III A	**IPSILATERAL** involvement of the mediastinal/subcarinal LN or chest wall	**SURGERY**

III **B**	**CONTRALATERAL** mets…	**C**hemo+XRT
	(*Remember,* "**B**" →"**B**ilateral " & **C**ontralateral → **C**hemo) …OR supraclavicular mets!)	
IV	Distant disease (as always)	Chemo+XRT

SMALL CELL Lung Ca

"Limited Disease" = Stages I-IIIA*   →   **Chemo** *** +XRT**

Extensive Disease"= Metastases   →   **Chemo only**

* **Limited disease, defined as disease confined to the**
ipsilateral hemithorax and within a single radiotherapy port.

** Commonly, **_cisplatin and etoposide_**

LYMPHOPROLIFERATIVE DISORDERS: <u>4</u> Important Ones:

C$_a$**LL** <u>**4**</u> H$_e$**LP** (*disorders of clonal expansion of lymphocytes*): (maybe you'd like an onc consult?!)

C LL

4

H airy cell leukemia
L ymphoma (e.g., Hodgkin's disease, and NHL)
P lasma cell dyscrasias (hyperproliferation of immunoglobulin by plasma cells): Multiple myeloma, MGUS, Waldenstrom's macroglobulinemia, primary amyloidosis, and cryoglobulinemia.

MALIGNANCIES ASSOCIATED WITH AIDS: C.H.A.L.K.

C ervical carcinoma
H odgkin's Lymphomas {& other lymphomas: NHL, CNS lymphomas, T-cell lymphomas)
A nogenital carcinomas
L eiomyomas; leiomyosarcomas.
K aposi's sarcoma

MECKEL'S DIVERTICULUM: RULE OF 2'S

- ✓ 2:1 Male: Female ratio
- ✓ 2 complications: hemorrhage and perforation
- ✓ 2 types of ectopic tissue: gastric and pancreatic
- ✓ Confused with 2 other problems: ulcers and appendix
- ✓ 2% incidence on autopsies (i.e. affects 2% of population)
- ✓ Usually occurs within 2 feet of the ileocecal valve
- ✓ Usually presents within the first 2 years of life
- ✓ Usually about 2 inches in length

MEN I Syndrome[1] (Multiple Endocrine Neoplasia)—aka Wermer Syndrome

1. Pituitary tumors
2. <u>Parathyroid tumor</u>
3. Pancreatic ca

> [1] THINK OF → <u>1 MAN (MEN I)</u> in a <u>panic</u> (panc) in his <u>parachute</u> (parathyroid) over <u>Pittsburgh</u> (pituitary tumor)

MEN <u>II</u>A Syndrome[2]—aka Sipple Syndrome

1. Pheo—remember, you have "**II**" adrenals (and in fact, the pheo in Sipple's is usually bilateral)
2. <u>Parathyroid tumor</u>
3. Medu**ll**ary thyroid ca

> [2] THINK OF → a "**Pair of** (Parathyroid) **medium** (medullary) **feet** (pheo)". **Even more beautiful** is that a **Pair = 2 (ie II) AND Feet = 2 (ie II)** !

MELANOMA: WORRY SIGNS FOR HYPERPIGMENTED LESIONS: ABCDE

A symmetry
B order is irregular—edges irregularly scalloped
C olor—mottled / variegated; may include shades of brown, black grey, red, and white
D iameter—greater than 6.0mm (roughly the size of a pencil eraser)
E nlargement—the patient's history of an ↑ in the size of the lesion <u>E</u>levation

> ✪ *Not to be confused with the above* **6mm** *(!), you should know that the best independent predictor of survival is the thickness of the melanoma on biopsy, and that thickness you hope is* ≤**.76mm** *for high chance of survival.*

Just as the first thing you do in Metaboli Acidosis is check for an Anion Gap, so in **METABOLIC ALKALOSIS ☞ you check the URINE CHLORIDE**. ***For the boards*** :

➢ A <u>Urine Chloride < 10</u> points to <u>surreptious vomiting</u> (loss of HCl yields a met alk)

➢ A <u>Urine Chloride > 10</u> points to <u>Bartter's syndrome</u> and <u>diuretics</u>.

✪ LABORATORY COMPARISON OF COMMON METABOLIC BONE DISEASES:

BONE DISORDER	SERUM CALCIUM	SERUM PHOSPHORUS	SERUM ALK PHOS
Osteoporosis	NL	NL	NL
Osteomalacia	↓	↓	↑
Hyperparathyroidism	↑	↓	↑
Renal failure/ osteodystrophy	↓	↑	↑
Paget's Disease	NL	NL	↑↑

MONOCLONAL GAMMOPATHY OF UNDETERMINED SIGNIFICANCE (MGUS):

When M-protein is detected on immunofixation, yet the clinical situation is "CALM", think of MGUS :

CALM implies you've ruled out …

C ryoglobulinemia

A myloidosis

L ymphoproliferative disorders (other)

M ultiple myeloma; Macroglobulinemia (Waldenstrom's)

- ➤ Specifically, *there is no:* anemia, no renal failure, no lytic lesions, no hypercalcemia, and no urinary Bence Jones proteins.
- ➤ M protein < 3g/dL
- ➤ Plasma cells in the bone marrow ≤ 10%
- ➤ Remember, I long-term follow-up shows that approximately 25 percent of patients with MGUS eventually transform into myeloma, patients with MGUS pe se require no therapy, and survival, on average is only about 2 years shorter than age-matched controls without MGUS.

KEY PHYSICAL FINDINGS IN MITRAL STENOSIS: "Pretty Loud DEMO"

P **re**systolic augmentation of the rumble

L **oud** S1

D iastolic rumble that increases with exercise and is heard best in the left lateral decubitus position

E levated JVD

M alar flush

O pening snap

SACRED PRINCIPLES OF MANAGEMENT IN MITRAL STENOSIS:

S urgery (open commisurotomy) is indicated in the symptomatic patient with pure MS whose effective orifice is < 1.0 cm^2. Over half of all patients undergoing mitral valvulotomy require reoperation by 10 years. Patients considered for MVR should have critical MS, i.e., an orifice < 0.6 cm^2/m^2 body surface area and be in the NYHA class III, i.e., symptomatic with ordinary activity, despite optimal medical therapy.

A nticoagulation (if AF or have evidence of pulmonary or systemic embolization)

C losed commisurotomy (percutaneous balloon valvuloplasty)

R ate control for patients in AF

E ndocarditis prophylaxis

D iuretics

MRI FOR THE BOARDS: IMPORTANT INDICATIONS

"That's 'S' as in 'S.C.A.N.' "

S eptic discitis

S teroids (chronic use) in a patient with hip or shoulder pain (for the boards) → avascular (aka aseptic) necrosis. The femoral head is a classic location.
Sickle cell, SLE, and alcoholism, and are other important risk factors for avascular necrosis.

S pinal/paraspinal abscess

S pinal stenosis (aka neural claudication)

S uspected cord compression (esp in cancer patients presenting with back pain/lower extremity weakness/incontinence/sacral paresthesias/etc, back pain being the #1 presenting symptom of cord compression in these patients)

MULTIPLE MYELOMA—KEY FEATURES #1: CARPE DIEM !

C alcium ↑; Cord compression (should be suspected in patients with severe back pain, weakness or paresthesias of the lower extremities, or bladder or bowel dysfunction or incontinence); Creatinine ↑ in ½ of patients at diagnosis

A nemia (normocytic, normochromic) in 2/3rds of patients → weakness & fatigue

R ouleau formation on PBS; Renal insufficiency

P lasma cells in the bone marrow > 10%; Plasmacytomas; "Punched out" (osteolytic) bone lesions[1] 2° to OAF (osteoclast-activating factor)—invisible on bone scan since no new bone formation occurs; Pain in the bones; Protein (total serum) ↑

E lectropheresis (SPEP & UPEP) and immunofixation[2] (for M-protein) important in diagnosis

D ecreased anion gap [i.e., $Na^{+\sim}$ ($\tilde{Cl}$ + $\tilde{HCO_3}$)] often noted because the M protein is cationic, resulting in retention of chloride for compensation.

I nfections, recurrent bacterial, esp. Strep pneumococcus & gram-negative infections, particularly during chemotherapy; Immunoglobulin deficiency

E SR ↑; Etiology unknown

M protein (= Monoclonal protein[3]; correlates to M-spike on SPEP/UPEP) is > 3g/dl. (*80% of patients;* the other 20% will only have light chains (Bence Jones proteins), which of course, must be measured in a 24-hour urine collection. Melphalan and prednisone are commonly used in the *treatment* of this incurable disease, since it's the least toxic and least expensive regimen. Treatment should be delayed until *either* evidence of progression or imminent complications.

1. Conventional radiographs reveal punched-out lytic lesions, osteoporosis, or fractures in nearly 80 percent of patients with multiple myeloma at diagnosis.
2. Immunofixation is critical for the differentiation of a monoclonal from a polyclonal "spike" in immunoglobulins and hence often follows the SPEP in order to ascertain the presence of an M-protein and to determine its type.
3. The most important diagnostic finding is the demonstration of a monoclonal (M) protein in the serum and/or urine in 98 percent of patients. Serum protein electrophoresis (SPEP) shows a localized band or peak in 80 percent, while immunofixation of the urine reveals an M protein in approximately 75 percent.

MULTIPLE MYELOMA—KEY FEATURES (#2):   CALCIUM

C alcium ↑

A nemia, normochromic normocytic

L ight chains, kappa and lambda

C ord compression

I nsufficiency, renal

U PEP, SPEP

M Protein

MYELOMA KIDNEY: **MECHANISMS OF RENAL INSUFFICIENCY:**   **U CLAP**

(you will when you see this on the exam):

U ric acid ↑, serum→ uric acid crystallization within the collecting tubules

C alcium ↑, serum (most common cause)

L ight chain deposition disease

A myloidosis

P lasma cell infiltration

MUSCULOSKELETAL DISORDERS ASSOCIATED WITH MALIGNANCY:

VOTED ALL CORPS

V   asculitis

A   rthritis

L   eukemia

L   ymphoma

C   arcinomatous polyarthritis

O   steoarthropathy (HPOA, hypertrophic pulmonary osteoarthropathy)

R   SD (Reflex Sympathetic Dystrophy), RA

P   olymyositis, Panniculitis, Paget's disease

S   jogren's, Scleroderma

CLINICAL CORRELATES OF MVP: RAW HEMP

R heumatic heart disease

A SD, secundum

W PW

H ypertrophic cardiomyopathy

E hlers-Danlos syndrome

M arfan's syndrome

P olycystic kidney disease; PCO; PAN; Postvalvulotomy

MYASTHENIA GRAVIS: WE ARE TIRED!

W eakness increases during repeated use (as opposed to Eaton-Lambert Syndrome, where it improves), and the patient typically complains of weakness that increases as the day progresses. Weakness in chewing is most noticeable after prolonged effort, as in chewing meat; facial muscle weakness

E asy fatiguability

A cquired weakness of the skeletal muscle that is due to autoimmune...
Acetylcholine receptor antibodies interfering with normal acetylcholine stimulation at the postsynaptic membrane at the neuromuscular junction. Acetylcholine receptor antibodies have a 90% sensitivity (70% in ocular myasthenia)
Antibodies to striated muscle (StrAb; aka antiskeletal muscle Ab) is highly associated with thymoma. It is most useful as a marker of thymoma in patients with MG onset before age 40, and is useful for following tumor recurrence post-thymectomy. Finally, it is a valuable marker in middle-aged or elderly patients with mild MG, where acetylcholine receptor antibodies are less likely to be positive.

R espiratory weakness (myasthenic crisis)

E aton Lambert Syndrome is the most important differential (esp. on exams)

T hymoma in 15% of MG patients. Of patients with thymoma, on the other hand, 50% have MG
Tensilon test used for confirmation. Tensilon is the short-acting acetylcholinesterase inhibitor edrophonium → in MG, usually see improvement of symptoms at the bedside in a minute or so.
Treatment
- PO acetylcholinesterase inhibitors, like neostigmine (Prostigmin®) or pyridostigmine (Mestinon®)
- High-dose steroids for severe attacks
- Plasmapheresis for severe, life-threatening cases.

I mprovement after thymectomy (in the absence of thymoma), in up to 85 % of patients; and of these, approx 35 % achieve drug-free remission. The concensus today is that thymectomy should be carried out in all patients with generalized MG between the ages of puberty and at least 55 years. The improvement in MG that is seen following thymectomy is delayed by ≥ 6 months)

R ecurrent aspiration pneumonias (2° to Dysphagia—*see below*).

E MG → should see a decremental response to repetitive stimulation ('post-tetanic inhibition') on the EMG

D iplopia (± ptosis; 20% of MG patients have only ocular myasthenia); Dysarthria; Dysphagia; Dyspnea

MYCOPLASMA PNEUMONIAE: M.P. MENACE

M ononeuritis multiplex

P resentation, usual: young patient with fever/dry cough/patchy bilateral interstitial infiltrates and a relatively benign exam.

M ilitary recruits; college kids

E rythema multiforme / Stevens-Johnson Syndrome

N onspecific symptoms: headache, malaise, low grade fever, chills, cough

A nemia, hemolytic: usually not severe

C ommunity-acquired pneumonia, esp in young patients
Cold agglutinin production: 60% of cases
CNS involvement: Guillain-Barre, cranial nerve palsies, polio-like syndrome, aseptic meningitis.

E rythromycin or doxycycline are the drugs of choice. Don't give PCN.

MYELOFIBROSIS: SPLEEN TIP

S plenomegaly[1]

P ancytopenia

L eukoerythroblastic[2] PBS

E xtramedullary hematopoiesis[1] (EMH)

E levations in: alk phos; leukocyte alk phos; uric acid; LDH; serum B12

N o specific therapy for idiopathic or 'agnogenic' myelofibrosis

T eardrop cells; Transformation into AML frequently

I nfections a major complication

P latelets show abnormal morphology; Palliative care generally since there is no specific therapy for idiopathic myelofibrosis

1. Splenomegaly and Hepatomegaly are both due to EMH.
2. Nucleated, ie premature, RBCs and early myeloid forms including blasts on peripheral blood smear (PBS)

MYOCARDIAL INFARCTIONS—INTERVENTIONS SHOWN TO ↓ MORTALITY:

PABST

P TCA

A SA / Antiplatelet agents, ACE inhibitors

B eta-blockers

S tatins, Spironolactone (if comorbid Grade III or IV NYHA CHF), Surgery

T hrombolytics

"NAIL YOUR LINES": *Here's how*:

➢ **MUehrcke's** LINES → Hypoalbuminemia associated with nephrotic syndrome. *(might think "u" for "urine" or "murky" (cloudy) urine)*

➢ **Mee's** LINES (white bands) → Arsenic poisoning *(as in "poisoning Me")*

➢ **Beau's** LINES → Transverse furrows or ridges of the nail plate that develop after dz or chemo and caused by temporary arrest of nail plate function *(imagine the furrows or ridges or worry lines on the brow of a guy named Beau after he got arrested)*

NON-ANION GAP ACIDOSIS: CRAP

C rap (diarrhea)

R TA's (Renal Tubular Acidoses)

A cetazolamide (carbonic anhydrase inhibitors); Adrenal insufficiency; Ammonium chloride

P arenteral nutrition; Posthypercapnia; Parathyroid ↑; Pancreatic fistula

NEPHROLOGY PEARLS YOU GOTTA KNOW:

✪ **NEPHROTIC SYNDROME**

➢ See ≥3.5g protein/24h urine; proteinuria→↓albumin→edema; ↑chol

➢ Proteinuria→Antithrombin III deficiency (a protein important in anticoag)→renal vein thrombosis (RVT)→thrombemboli can be seen→pulmonary emboli.

✪ **Muddy brown casts** → ATN (Acute tubular necrosis)

✪ **Acute Interstitial nephritis** 2° to drug hypersensitivity →check Hansel's stain for **urine eosinophils**. Common **medications** that can cause AIN include: β-lactam antibiotics NSAIDs sulfa antibiotics thiazide diuretics

✪ The #1 cause of **Glomerulonephritis** (GN) and the #1 cause of incidental microscopic hematuria is IgA Nephropathy (Berger's Disease); there is no proven treatment for IgA nephropathy.

✪ In differentiating **GN following URI**, remember the timing is important: Poststreptococcal GN averages 10 days after pharyngitis and 21 days after impetigo. This is in contrast to IgA Nephropathy, which typically occurs 3-5 days after URI or GI infection.

✪ **Rhabdomyolysis**: labs: ↑CPK,↑K+, ↑U.A., ↑Phos→↓Ca, and ↑creat may be seen if myoglobinuria develops; if urine dipstick + for heme (Hgb or Mgb) and yet few or no RBCs→suspect myoglobinuric renal failure.

✪ If you see **RBC casts** → Think **glomerular** nephritis

If you see **WBC/ WBC casts** → Think inflammation (e.g **interstitial** nephritis) or infection (e.g. **pyelo**nephritis); remember, the term "pyuria" means > 5 leukocytes per high power field

✪ **Contrast nephropathy** classically presents as an acute rise in BUN and creatinine with onset within 24 to 28 h, peaks 3 to 5 days, and resolves within a week.

✪ **KNOW THE DIFFERENCE** between **NEPHROTIC AND NEPHRITIC** presentations:

> ✪ <u>**Nephritis/nephritic syndrome**</u> usually requires RBC casts, hematuria (microscopic or macroscopic), and proteinuria, whereas **nephrotic syndrome** encompasses the constellation of proteinuria (>3.5g/24h)→ hypoalbuminemia → edema; and hyperlipidemia.

> ✪ <u>**Renal syndromes**</u> **can be <u>DIVIDED INTO</u>** ARF, RTAs, nephritic syndrome, and nephrotic syndrome. Just as **ARF** is classified in terms of prerenal/renal/postrenal and **RTAs** are classified into types 1,2, & 4, so nephritic and nephrotic syndromes have their subclassifications. <u>**Nephrotic**</u> syndromes are divided into **renal vs. systemic**. <u>**Nephritic**</u> syndromes are subclassified into **normal vs. low serum complement (C3)**.

GLOMERULOPATHY	✪ **KEY ASSOCIATIONS**
MEMBRANOPROLIFERATIVE (MPGN)	SLE, Sickle Cell, ↓C′
MINIMAL CHANGE Disease	*Hodgkins* Dz, NSAIDs, 80% respond to steroids
FOCAL SEGMENTAL Sclerosis	*HIV; heroine*
MEMBRANOUS	*Solid organ neoplasms*(esp lung, colon). Membranous yields renal vein thrombosis in 25-50% of cases. It is also the #1 cause of idiopathic nephrosis in adults
Note: Both <u>**Hep B**</u> and <u>**Hep C**</u> can cause **membranous, membranoproliferative,** and **diffuse proliferative** (classic post-infectious) GNs.	

NEPHR<u>O</u>TIC DISORDERS: BASIC FINDINGS: LEAP <u>O</u>ver

L ipids ↑
E dema
A lbumin ↓
P roteinuria

NEPHR<u>O</u>TIC SYNDROME—CAUSES: **O_H DAVID !**

D iabetes,
A myloidosis
V asculitis
I nfections
D rugs

NEPHRITIC DISORDERS: **PAIRS**

P ost-streptococcal GN

A lport's disease

I gA nephropathy

R apidly progressive GN (RPGN)

S LE

COMPLEMENT LEVELS IN NEPHRITIC AND NEPHROTIC SYNDROMES:

	↓ Serum C′	Normal Serum C′
PRIMARY renal dz	**P**oststrep GN **M**PGN (membranoproliferative) **You lie 'down in PM'**	**B**erger's Dz (IgA) **A**lport's Syndrome **R**PGN (p- or c-ANCA+) **'BAR none'**
SYSTEMIC disease	**S**LE **I**nfective Endocard **M**ixed essential cryo **'SLIM down'**	**G**oodpasture's Dz **H**US **O**ccult Abscess **S**ystemic Vasculitis (Wegener's; PAN; HSP) **T** T P **GHOST** (paranormal)

WHICH **CASTS** MEAN WHAT ?!	
✪ **TYPE of CAST**	**KEY CULPRITS**
RBC casts	➤ Acute GN ➤ Malignant HTN
WBC casts	➤ Pyelonephritis ➤ *Intersitital nephritis* (re: also WBCs and urine eos)
Hyaline	➤ *Prerenal azotemia;* ➤ HTN; often just normal
Pigmented granular casts, aka **"muddy brown"** casts	*ATN*
Fatty casts	*Nephrotic* syndrome
Waxy casts	*Chronic renal failure*

POOR PROGNOSTICATORS IN NON-HODGKINS LYMPHOMA: **ALE** on **TAP**

A nn Arbor stage III or IV (this system has some value in NHL too)
L DH (elevated)
E xtranodal nodes: sites >1

on

T umor burden*
A ge (>60)
P erformance status (ECOG ≥2). A score of 2 or above implies that patient requires rest for ≥ part of the day because of his or her disease, ie *not* "fully ambulatory".

* Tumor burden considers:
  - Systemic symptoms
  - ≥3 lymph nodes sites >3 cm
  - A single lymph node site >7 cm
  - Platelets <100,000/μL or absolute neutrophil count <1,000/μL
  - Circulating lymphoma cells >5,000/μL
  - Marked splenomegaly, compressive symptoms, pleural effusion, or ascites.

NEUROLEPTIC MALIGNANT SYNDROME (NMS):   NEUROLEPTICS

N   MS clinical features *include…*

E   ncephalopathy

U   nsteady gait (festinating gait)

R   igidity, cogwheel

O   culogyric crisis*

L   ead pipe muscle rigidity, Lockjaw (trismus)

E   xaggerated movement disorder (dyskinesia)

P   rominent diaphoresis

T   emperature > 100.4 ° F (38 °C) in the absence of any known cause,

Tachycardia, Tachypnea

I   ncreased BP, Incontinence

C   horeiform movements

S   ialorrhea (drooling), Swallowing difficulties (dysphagia)

* This acute dystonia involves a sudden but sustained maximal
deviation of the eyes, usually upward, that persists for several minutes or hours

The 4 *MAIN* clinical features, however, are: HARM

H   yperthermia

A   utonomic dysfunction (severe tachycardia, labile blood pressure,

profuse diaphoresis, dyspnea and respiratory insufficiency)

R   igidity (lead-pipe)

M   ental status changes

NORMAL PRESSURE HYDROCEPHALUS: AID

A   taxia

I   ncontinence

D   ementia

OBSTRUCTIVE SLEEP APNEA—CLINICAL FEATURES: PA SNORES !

P oorly rested on awakening; daytime drowsiness

A M Headaches; Apneic episodes, nocturnal → hypoxia → Arrhythmias
(ventricular)

S noring

N asal CPAP an important tool in treatment

O bstructive sleep apnea 2° to obesity, the disorder is referred to as
Pickwickian Syndrome

R VF (→ LVF in late stages); ↑ RBCs (polycythemia) secondary to
hypoxia

E dema, peripheral 2° to Pulm HTN/cor pulmonale

S ystemic / pulmonary hypertension

OCTREOTIDE INDICATIONS: Label & Off-Label Uses: D.I.A.B.E.T.E.S.*

D iarrhea due to AIDS (eg cryptosporidiosis, etc), chemotherapy, or
GVHD
Dumping syndrome (postgastrectomy)

I nsulinomas

A cromegaly; ACTH- producing tumors

B leeding esophageal varices; Breast carcinoma

E ndocrine tumors of the GI tract (glucagonoma; Zollinger-Ellison
syndrome; somatostatinoma; insulinoma—already listed; VIPoma
diarrhea)

T SH-secreting pituitary adenomas; Thyroid (medullary)—octreotide
scintigraphy

E nterocutaneous fistulas (established, but also prevention of such
fistulas post-pancreatectomy)

S ymptoms of carcinoid syndrome (flushing/diarrhea)

> *   ***Hyperglycemia is also common to all underlined disorders***

ORAL & GENITAL ULCERATION--DIFFERENTIAL: B.E.H.C.E.T.'S.

B	ehcet's syndrome	→	Painful
E.	multiforme	→	Painful
H	SV	→	Painful
C	rohn's disease	→	Pain*less*
E	pidermal bullae of pemphigus vulgarus	→	Painful
T	riad of Reiter's	→	Pain*less*
S	yphilis	→	Pain*less*

IMPORTANT OCULOMUCOCUTANEOUS SYNDROMES: SUPERB !

S   weet's syndrome

U   lcerative colitis

P   emphigus vulgarus (& cicatrical pemphigoid)

E   rythema Multiforme

R   eiter's syndrome

B   ehcet's syndrome

ORAL LEUKOPLAKIA: PERSISTS

P <u>remalignant</u> lesion--approximately 10% of lesions can progress to malignancy.

E tiology: caused by exposure to the same agents that cause squamous cell ca: <u>smoking</u>, <u>alcohol</u>, chronic irritation/inflammation, <u>HPV-16, & HPV-18</u>.

R ubbing / scraping it does not remove the lesion. It *persists* even after the irritation (e.g. smoking) has been stopped for several weeks.

S harply-defined, white, macular or slightly raised area in the mouth.

I nvasion, secondary, by candida common

S erious when the leukoplakia involves the <u>tongue or floor of the mouth</u>, with over 60% showing either carcinoma in situ or invasive SCC whereas buccal involvement is almost always benign.

T he most common precancerous lesion of the oral mucosa, representing 85% of such lesions. It is also the most common of all chronic lesions of the oral mucosa, affecting 3% of white adults.

S moking and alcohol markedly increase the chance of malignant *transformation*. When seen together, they are Synergistic as such. Seventy-ninety percent of leukoplakia patients are smokers. Stopping smoking results in either regression or the complete disappearance (58%) in 78% of patients at 12 months. Surgical excision remains the treatment of choice for small leukoplakias. The key is long-term follow-up after removal, because recurrences are frequent and additional leukoplakias occur. Clinical evaluation every six months is recommended.

OSGOOD-SCHLATTERS DISEASE: EXCRUTIATING

E piphysitis seen exclusively in young men > women whose growth centers are still active. Exam: Extending the knee against resistance, stressing the quadriceps, or squatting with the knee in full flexion.

X rays often instrumental in dx

C alcified thickening at the tendonous insertion of the patella.

R elief of symptoms occurs with rest or restriction of activities.

U sually unilateral (75%)

C auses: trauma and exercise are common precipitants (Chronic microtrauma to the tibial tuberosity secondary to overuse of the quadriceps muscle is a leading theory of etiology.)

 I rregular ossification of the proximal tibial tuberosity (insertion point of quadriceps)

A dolescents most common; age typically < 19yo. Girls who are affected are typically aged 10-11 years. Boys who are affected are typically aged 13-14 years.

T ibial tuberosity osteochondritis frequently noted on radiographs

 I nitial treatment should include Ice x 20 minutes q 2-4 h; Infrapatellar strap during activity; a knee Immobilizer for a few days may improve compliance, especially in more severe cases.

N SAIDs, in addition to rest, for general management; usually remits spontaneously; steroids if persists

G ender difference: M>>F

OSMOLAR GAP= 2[Na+] + [Glucose/18] + [BUN/2.8] . Greater than 10 is abnormal. Osmolar Gap= the measured osmolarity (lab) - your calculated osmolarity.

✪ Main causes are alcohols (generally end in -*OLS*) ⇒ methan**OL**; ethan**OL**; ethylene glyc**OL**; isopropyl alcoh**OL**; mannit**OL**; and acetone.

✪ Know that **_ethylene glycol_** (antifreeze) gives <u>calcium oxalate crystals</u>.
✪ Know that **_isopropyl_** *alcohol* (rubbing alcohol) causes ketones, and an osmolar gap but NOT an anion gap.

OSTEOARTHRITIS—RADIOGRAPHIC SIGNS: Bone LOSS

L oss of joint space
O steophytosis
S ubchondral cysts
S ubchondral sclerosis

OSTEOMALACIA—Important Causes: I.D. AFGHAN CAMPS

I nadequate sunlight exposure
D ietary deficiency in vitamin D or calcium

A ntacids (can lead to phosphate deficiency)
F anconi Syndrome (leads to impaired phosphate reabsorption; eg Wilsons disease, multiple myeloma)
G astrectomy
H ypoparathyroidism (1°); <u>H</u>yperparathyroidism { (2°); eg RTA, Type I and disorders of vit D metabolism}; <u>H</u>ypoPhosphatasia
A luminum, bisphosphonates—inhibitors of mineralization
N ephrotic syndrome (loss of vit D-binding protein)

C RF; <u>C</u>irrhosis (biliary; <u>alcoholic</u>)
A nticonvulsants (adversely affect vit D metabolism)
M alabsorption
P ancreatic insufficiency
S mall bowel disease

OSTEOMALACIA: Key Features: **PALM PDA**

P roximal RTA (Type II) → Phosphate[1] wasting; *calcium* (serum) ↓ to low-normal due to the metabolic acidosis (when osteomalacia is due to vit D deficiency with 2° hyperparathyroidism)

A lk phos ↑ (when osteomalacia is due to vit D deficiency with 2° hyperparathyroidism); alk phos ↓ when osteomalacia is 2° to hypophosphatasia

L ooser zones (pseudofractures)[2]—these are fissures, or narrow radiolucent lines, two to five mm in width with sclerotic borders, are the characteristic radiologic finding in osteomalacia

M echanisms: 1) Mineralization failure; 2) abnormal vit D metabolism; and 3) phosphate deficiency; Management includes calcium + vitamin D

P arathyroidism (2° hyperparathyroidism) → renal osteodystrophy[3]

D eficient vitamin D (absorption, production, resistance)

A ka "rickets" in children

1. Among the different causes of osteomalacia and osteoporosis, serum phosphate is low in the following scenarios: a) vit D deficiency with 2° hyperparathyroidism; b) conditions associated with urinary wasting; and c) proximal RTA

2. It is unknown whether Looser zones represent stress fractures (which have been   repaired by the laying down of inadequately mineralized osteoid), or represent erosion by arterial pulsations since they often lie in apposition to arteries.

3. In this setting, proximal phosphate wasting, increased calcium loss due to the metabolic acidosis, and secondary hyperparathyroidism may all contribute to the decrease in bone mineralization.

OSTEOPOROSIS—RISK FACTORS: **M/F CLASH**   <u>or</u>   **OSTEOPATH**

M alignancy

F amily history; Fracture history

C orticosteroids

L ow: calcium intake/body weight (< 127 lb)/Estrogen/activity (sedentary lifestyle)

A lcohol, Advanced Age

S moking

H igh: T4/ PTH/glucose (DM)/corticosteroids; Hypogonadism (low T or E) Heparin, prolonged

or …

O steopenia

S teroids; Smoking; Sugar (DM)

T hyrotoxicosis

E ndocrine (thyrotoxicosis, hyperparathyroidism, diabetes mellitus, Cushing's syndrome)

O ld (prior) fracture between the ages of 20 and 50 years

P rolonged immobilization; ↑PTH;

A lcohol; Above average height; Absorption of vit D and/or calcium ↓

T umor

H ypogonadism; Heparin (prolonged)

P. VERA—Key FEATURES: PHLEBOTOMY

P hlebotomy important in treatment (except for patients over 60 who are not high risk); Pruritis (aquagenic); facial Plethora; Peptic ulcer disease

H yperviscosity-related symptoms; Hepato/splenomegaly

L AP score ↑; Leukocytosis

E po levels ↓; Erythrocytosis; Erythromelalgia (painful redness of the extremities)

B 12 frequently ↑

O verproduction of phenotypically normal red cells, granulocytes, & platelets in the absence of a recognizable physiologic stimulus (P. Vera)

T hrombotic complications (eg Budd-Chiari Syndrome)—the major cause of death ☞ About 25-30% of patients present with a thrombotic event (CVA, MI, DVT, portal vein thrombosis) and 30-40% of all PV patients eventually die from a thrombotic or hemorrhagic event. Thrombocytosis; Transformation to AML & myelofibrosis with myeloid metaplasia in patients treated with chemo.

O xygen saturation ↑

M ass (RBC) ↑

Y ears: 60 yo = median age at diagnosis.

PAGET'S DISEASE OF THE BONE: C. PAINS!

C   ardiac failure (high ouput)

P   ain in the long bones

A   rthralgias; Axial skeleton > Appendicular skeleton affected, so spine, sacrum, pelvis, femur, tibia are the major bones affected)

I   ncreased alk phos

N   ormal serum calcium (!); Nerve compression; Neural deafness; N-telopeptide (urinary) helpful in diagnosis; Nuclear bone scans see "hot" spots of Paget's dz, and are far better than plain films in dx; Neoplastic transformation, esp tumors fo the humerus and femur

S   kull (lytic lesions here called osteoporosis circumscripta)

PAGET'S DISEASE: PAGET'S CONT'D

P   athologic fractures due to weakened, disorganized bone structure; Pain, skeletal

A   lk phos ↑(similar to osteomalacia) and it correlates with disease activity.

G   enetic factors play a significant role. From 15-25 % of family members of patients with Paget's will eventually contract the disease. Also, first degree relatives of Paget's patients have a sevenfold increase in going on to develop the disease.

E   ighth cranial nerve compressed by enlarging bone, resulting in hearing loss, is a well-recognized potential neurologic complications, most of which are caused by nerve compression by enlarging bone or by interference with the blood supply.

T   umorous transformation (malignant potential), esp osteosarcomas of the humerus and femur

S   keleton affected is axial >> appendicular, with particular preference for: long bones (femur, tibia, humerus), pelvis, spine, sacrum, & skull (lytic lesions here called osteoporosis circumscripta)

C ardiac complications include: CHF ("high output cardiac failure"); valvular stenosis; conduction abnormalities

O steogenic sarcomas (osteosarcomas) are the most common tumors and are found most frequently in the pelvis, femur, humerus, skull, and facial bones

N uclear bone scans see "hot" spots of Paget's dz, and are far better than plain films in dx-- the most sensitive test in identifying pagetic bone lesions.
N-telopeptide (urinary) are very useful markers; Normal serum Ca (similar to osteoporosis), except with immobilization

T reatment—calcitonin; bisphosphonates (eg alendronate, pamidronate, tiludronate, risedronate); gallium nitrate

D isorganized bone remodeling→ bone is structurally weakened; Deformities ("bowing" of femurs).

DIFFERENTIAL DIAGNOSIS OF PALPABLE PURPURA: CRIBSHEET

C holesterol emboli

R heumatoid arthritis

I nfectious emboli (e.g. meningococcus; GC; rickettsiae, eg Rocky Mt Spotted Fever)

B & C hepatitis

S mall vessel vasculitides → Microscopic polyangiitis, PAN; Wegener's; Goodpasture's; Churg-Strauss; and Behcet's.
RA, Cryoglobulinemia, HSP would also fall here.

H SP; HIV; "Hypersensitivity Vasculitis"

E cthyma gangrenosum

E ssential, mixed cryoglobulinemia

T emporal arteritis; Tumor emboli (eg atrial myxoma)

CLINICAL FEATURES OF ACUTE PANCREATITIS: AMYLASE

A cute pain; Alcohol is the #1 cause (acute on chronic) and gallstones are #2.

M id-abdominal staining (Grey Turner's and Cullen's signs)—loin and periumbilical respectively

Y ellow (ascites)

L ipase ↑; Left-sided pleural effusion

A mylase ↑ (usu. > 1000)

S entinel loop (Small bowel ileus overlying the pancreatic area)

E mesis and nausea

RANSON'S CRITERIA: POOR PROGNOSTICATORS IN ACUTE PANCREATITIS

AT TIME OF ADMISSION OR DIAGNOSIS:

"Andre Will Golf Laguna Soon"

A ge > 55yo
W BC >16
G lucose (serum) > 200
L DH > 350
S GOT (AST) > 250 IU/L

DURING INITIAL 48 HOURS:

"Ranson's **BASeline BUNdle Sure CAn Help Out"**

B ase deficit > 4 mEq/L   4
B UN increase of > 5 mg/dl   5
S equestration of fluid > 6 L   6
C alcium < 8 mg/dl   8
H ct decrease > 10%   10
O xygen < 60 mm Hg   60

CLINICAL FEATURES OF CHRONIC PANCREATITIS: C MAIDS
(think 'C' for chronic as in "old maids!")

C alcification, pancreatic; Chronic (!)

M alabsorption
A bdominal pain (Alcohol is the #1 cause, similar to AP)
I cterus
D iabetes
S teatorrhea

KEY DRUGS that can cause PANCREATITIS: **"PD FAST VET"**
         (as in "Pretty Fast corVETte"):

P   entamidine

D   idanosine (ddI)

F   urosemide

A   zathioprine

S   ulfa

T   hiazides

V   alproic acid

E   strogen

T   etracycline

PARACENTESIS:

Transudates	**EXudates** (also, *everything EXceeds**)
CHF/cirrhosis/nephrosis	TB (infEXtion)
Portal HTN	Fungal (infEXtion)
↓Albumin	SBP (infEXtion)
Meig's Syndrome	Cancers (e.g. hepatoma; mesothelioma; mets; ovarian) ("My EX"!)

CAUSES OF TRANSUDATIVE EFFUSIONS: **MUNCHES**

M   yxedema

U   rinothorax

N   ephrotic syndrome

C   irrhosis

H   eart failure

E   mboli, Pulmonary

S   uperior Vena Cava obstruction

IMPORTANT PARACENTESIS LABS TO REMEMBER: 5C's:

C ell count and differential
C oncentration of albumin and total protein/amylase/glucose/LDH
C ultures

And, especially if <u>malignant</u> ascites is suspected, …

C ytology
C EA

PARVOVIRUS B19:   SLAP CHEEK

S lapped cheek appearance = the erythematous, malar rash (erythema infectiosum—also below) of fifth disease

L acelike, reticulated rash on the trunk and extremities is the other type of rash that is common in B19

A plastic crisis, transient--Parvovirus B19 infection is the cause in most instances of transient aplastic crisis developing suddenly in patients with chronic hemolytic disease
<u>A</u>symptomatic infection—the most common clinical manifestation; as many as 25 percent of persons have no symptoms at all, and 50 percent have no symptoms characteristic of B19

P olyarthropathy-- Usually symmetric; most commonly involve the hands, wrists, knees, and feet; usually resolves within a few weeks; does not cause joint destruction; (giant) <u>P</u>ronormoblasts

C hronic infection with anemia in immunocompromised patients; <u>C</u>hronic infection without anemia

H ydrops fetalis

E rythema infectiosum

E rythrocyte aplasia (aka pure RBC aplasia)

K inds of hemolytic anemias that B19 can complicate: most any: including sickle cell disease, erythrocyte enzyme deficiencies, hereditary spherocytosis, thalassemias, paroxysmal nocturnal hemoglobinuria, and autoimmune hemolysis.

IMPORTANT CAUSES OF PATHOLOGICAL 'Q' WAVES: KIMCHI PIE
(≥1mm wide (.04s) or ≥ one-third of the entire QRS amplitude)

K $^{+}$ ↑
I schemia without infarction
M yocarditis
C ardiomyopathy, hyptertrophic; Conduction problems: LBBB
H ypertrophy, ventricular-- left or right
I nappropriate lead placement

P re-excitation (eg WPW → 'Pseudoinfarction')
I nfarction, transmural
E mbolus, pulmonary

PEA (Pulseless Electrical Activity): Reversible Causes With Acute Interventions:

5-HT$_4$ (as in the newer serotonin drugs for IBS)

H ypovolemia → bolus IV fluids
H ypoxia → hyperventilate
H ydrogen ion excess—acidosis → hyperventilate
H yperkalemia/H ypokalemia → as appropriate
H ypothermia (eg if see Osborne waves) → rewarm

T hrombosis (PE and coronary) → thrombolysis for PE
T ension pneumothorax →chest tube
T amponade → pericardiocentesis
T ablets (drug overdose) → as appropriate

PELIOSIS HEPATIS*—CLINICAL ASSOCIATIONS: CAPO

C at-scratch disease and bacillary angiomatosis (Bartonella henselae=causative organism)
A nabolic steroids
P regnancy
O CPs

* Describes blood-filled cysts in the liver

PEMPHIGUS VULGARIS: ALOT OF PAINS

A norexia & dysphagia (see 'Oral lesions' below) can lead to significant weight loss
Acute or chronic (versus Bullous Pemphigoid (BP) which is chronic only)

L ymphomas & leukemias often predate pemphigus. In such cases where the mucocutaneous condition is caused by the underlying internal malignancy, this is referred to as paraneoplastic pemphigus

O ral lesions: initiall presentation in 60%; 80-90% of all PV patients will eventually have oral lesions; interval = 6 months b/w onset of oral lesions and dissemination to skin

T hymoma / myasthenia commonly associated

O ften life-threatening

F laccid, superficial bullae (blisters) on non-inflamed skin; rupture leads to large erosions; bullae have usually ruptured by time of presentation; by contrast, bullae in BP are usually tense and intact

P eak incidence between 4th & 6th decades of life (versus 6th & 8th for BP)
Painful oral & skin lesions
Penicillamine, captopril, and enalopril are some commonly used drugs which can trigger this auto-immune disease. In penicillamine use, the eruption may not develop until 6 months after the onset of therapy. Drug-induced cases of PV resolve after the drug is discontinued.

A utoantibodies to intercellular substance

I ntraepidermal blister

N ikolsky's sign: application of pressure to blister causes extension of bullae

S teroids & immunosuppressives to treat

PERIPHERAL NEUROPATHIES—DIFFERENTIAL: DIABETES

D iabetes

I nfectious (Lyme dz, HIV, Guillain-Barre, etc)

A myloidosis

B 12 deficiency; Blood disorders (multiple myeloma; MGUS; P vera; cryoglobulinemia)

E thanol

T oxic, eg arsenic; organophosphates; lead; thallium; mercury; methyl bromide

E ndocrine (eg thyroid)

S arcoidosis

PERNICIOUS ANEMIA—LABS: **"MAMA HAS** pernicious anemia."

M acrocytic anemia / ↑MCV
A nemia
M ethylmalonic acid ↑
A nti-intrinsic factor antibody +

H omocysteine ↑
A nti-parietal cell Ab +
S chilling test +

PEUTZ-JEGHERS DISEASE: "P&J or **H.A.M.**?"

H amartomatous polyps (small intestine > colon > stomach > rectum): these polyps can produce symptoms (pain, obstruction, bleeding) or undergo malignant transformation (2-3% risk of malignant transformation)*.
A utosomal dominant
M ucocutaneous pigmentation (melanin spots of the buccal mucosa/lips/fingers/toes present in more than 95 %); Malignancy risk ↑ (GI tumors: greatest for small intestine, then stomach and colon; ↑ risk of NON-GI tumors ** as well)

*   Beyond this commonly quoted small risk of transformation, _coexisting adenomas_ lead to a marked increased prevalence of adenocarcinoma. In fact, relative to the lifetime risk for sporadic colorectal cancer in the United States (about 5%), patients with PJS have a 4 -to-12-fold elevated risk of developing colorectal carcinoma.

**   _Giardiello and colleagues_ [1] found a relative risk for cancer 18 times that of the general population in 31 PJS patients. Malignancies involved pancreas (4), breast (2), stomach (2), colon (2), lung (2), and endometrium (1). _Spigelman and colleagues_ [2] reported that 72 retrospectively studied PJS patients were 13 times more likely than the general population to develop a malignancy.

[1] Giardiello FM, Welsh SB, Hamilton SR, et al. Increased risk of cancer in the Peutz-Jeghers syndrome. N Engl J Med 1987;316:1511–1514.

[2] Spigelman AD, Murray V, Phillips RKS. Cancer and the Peutz-Jeghers syndrome. Gut 1989;30:1588–1590.

PHEOCHROMOCYTOMA: *RULE OF 10's:*

10% of pheos are extraadrenal
10% are malignant
10% are familial
10% are bilateral (since familial tumors tend to be bilateral)

PITYRIASIS ROSEA: **HERPES**

H erald patch first appears (80% of patients), typically on the trunk, followed 1-2 weeks later by a generalized secondary eruption most often to the trunk and proximal extremities. The herald patch is typically an oval, slighlty raised plaque 2-5 cm, bright red, with a fine scale at the periphery; may be multiple. Herald patch commonly misdiagnosed as ringworm the herald patch can resemble tinea corporis so closely that KOH examination of scales for dermatophyte hyphae may be necessary to distinguish these conditions.

E tiology: HHV-8 (Human Herpesvirus-8)

R eassurance in most cases. Topical steroids in the middle potency range are helpful in the control of itching

P eak incidence: older children/young adults; ages 10-35 yo

E xcept for itching, the condition is usually asymptomatic.

S pontaneously remitting usually by 6 weeks; Spring and fall especially

PITYRIASIS VERSICOLOR (TINEA VERSICOLOR): **SPOT FACTS**

S paghetti and meatballs is the pattern that's described on KOH prep, as it reveals both hyphae and spores

P revention: Topical selenium sulfide solution 2.5 percent (Selsun) applied to the entire body for ten minutes every two to three weeks is effective, as is oral ketoconazole (400 mg once per month) and itraconazole (200 mg twice daily for one day per month).

O vergrowth of the hyphal form of Pityrosporum ovale, a saprophytic yeast that is part of the normal skin flora.

T runk is typical location of these well-demarcated scaling macular "spots" with variable pigmentation, occurring most commonly on the.

F actors which can trigger conversion to the mycelial or hyphal form that is associated with clinical disease include: hot and humid weather, use of oils, hyperhidrosis, and immunosuppression.

A dolescents and young adults most commonly affected

C ortisol levels, when ↑, predispose individuals to PV (e.g. Cushing's or exogenous steroids)

<u>C</u>hronic, asymptomatic scaling dermatosis

T reatment: topical antifungal therapy is the treatment of choice for patients with limited disease. Virtually any topical anti-yeast preparation can be used with cure rates exceeding 70 to 80 percent. Treatment usually continues for two weeks. Ketoconazole as a single oral dose of 400 mg or 200 mg QD for five days achieves cure rates greater than 90 to 95 percent at four weeks.

S ummer most cases diagnosed because the organism produces azelaic acid, which inhibits the normal pigmentation process. Plus many of the major aggravating factors are present in summer ("hot and humid weather, use of oils, hyperhidrosis").

QUICK DIFFS ™

QUICK DIFFERENTIALS FOR PLEURAL FLUID ANALYSIS :

LOW GLUCOSE (less than 25 mg/100 mL):   **TRAMPLE** <u>down</u> **(<u>glu</u> OR <u>pH</u> !)**

T   B (don't forget pleural biopsy if suspect)
R   uptured esophagus (Boerhaave's syndrome)-esp with ↓pH and ↑amylase)
A   rthritis (RA) (esp. if also find ↓pH and ↑LDH)
M   alignancy
P   arapneumonic effusions; <u>P</u>erforated ulcer (for ↓ pH only
L   upus pleuritis
E   mpyema

AMYLASE ↑:   "<u>Amy</u>'s **PERM**"

P   ancreatitis, acute or chronic
E   mpyema
R   uptured esophagus
M   alignancy (10% of the time)

BLOODY PLEURAL FLUID: "<u>Bloody</u> **TAMP**on"
(sorry, but if it gets you an extra point on the exam…)

T   B; <u>T</u>raumatic tap
A   sbestosis
M   alignancy
P   ulmonary infarction

✪ **Remember also ADENOSINE DEAMINASE (ADA) in Tuberculosis:**
as in a <u>tube</u> of toothpaste (if you're in a real pinch!)

COMMON CAUSES OF MALIGNANT PLEURAL EFFUSIONS:

Meta S.L.O.B. or MO' LBS !

M etastases to the pleura; Mesothelioma

S tomach cancer (uncommon)
L ung cancer, Lymphoma (NHL: direct pleural involvement; HL: lymphatic obstruction)
O varian cancer (uncommon)
B reast cancer

LYMPHS PREDOMINATE (Nymphs predominate?): LiVe FAST!

L ymphoma
V iral

F ungal infection
A rthritis (RA)
S arcoidosis
T B

Eosinophils ↑ in Pleural Fluid: ABCD

A ir in the pleural space; Asbestosis
B lood in the pleural space
C hurg Strauss syndrome
D rugs (eg dantrolene, bromocryptine, nitrofurantoin)

PLUMMER-VINSON SYNDROME: DAMSEL

D ysphagia
A trophic pharyngitis; Achlorhydria
M icrocytic anemia; Malignant disposition
S plenomegaly
E sophageal webs
L adies, predilection

PML (Progressive Multifocal Leukoencephalopathy): WHITE OUT !

W hite matter disease of the CNS
H emiparesis
I ntellectual/cognitive decline
T reatment is simply combination HAART (Highly Active Anti-HIV Therapy)
E tiology: The JC virus, a slow virus, is responsible for PML. It is named after the initials of the first patient diagnosed with PML.More than 70% of all adults in the United States are infected with the JC virus, usually during early childhood. However, the virus only becomes active in people who have compromised immune systems.

O ptho: visual field deficits and progressively decreasing vision; Opportunistic infection, esp AIDS, lymphoma, leukemia
U nusual findings: aphasia, ataxia, cranial nerve deficits
T 2-weighted images on MRI are hyperintense (extra white)

IMPORTANT INDICATIONS FOR PNEUMOCOCCAL VACCINE: HE CRAMS

H odgkin's disease; HIV & other immunocompromised states (leukemia; bone marrow transplant; chemotherapy; long-term use of systemic steroids)
E ndocrine: diabetes

C hronic CSF leaks
R enal: CRF; nephrotic syndrome; renal transplant—all conditions associated with rapid antibody decline after initial vaccination
A lcoholic cirrhosis; Age ($\geq$ 65 yo)
M ultiple myeloma; Malignancy (generalized)
S pleen (hypo or asplenic)—eg Sickle cell disease

Polyarteritis Nodosa (PAN):   p-ANCA

P alpable purpura and livido reticularis;   'p-AN'CA (as opposed to Wegener's = c-ANCA →"We cAN"). However, in vasculitides, cannot rely on the ANCA for dx; need biopsy! Prednisone (high-dose); or cyclophosphamide + prednisone; Pain—abdominal and testicular (orchitis)
A bdominal aneurysms (eg celiac axis)
N eurologic complications: mononeuritis multiplex; asymmetric polyneuropathy; stroke; confusion. Necrotizing glomerulonephritis (focal) → leads to hypertension & renal insufficiency
C onstitutional symptoms: fatigue, weight loss, myalgia, fever Cardiac complications (Angina, MI, CHF) Commonly involved organs include: intestine, kidneys, skin (livedo reticularis, purpura, ulcers), peripheral nerves, and joints; the lungs are usually spared.
A rthralgias

POLYCYSTIC KIDNEY DISEASE:

HARLEM or PALM BEACH ? *(You choose!)*

H ypertension; Hematuria; Hepatic cysts
A neurysms, berry
R ecurrent: infections / renal calculi
L arge kidneys; Lumbar pain
E SRD (renal failure affects 1 in 4 by age 50 and 1 in 2 by age 70)
M VP

or

P ressure ↑
A neurysms, berry
L arge kidneys; Lumbar pain
M VP

B lacks have an ↑ incidence
E SRD
A lot of UTIs!
C alculi, renal
H ypertension; Hematuria; Hepatic cysts

POLYCYSTIC OVARIAN SYNDROME: OVARIAN

O besity
V irilization (hirsutism, clitorimegaly, ovarian and adrenal androgens ↑)
A menorrhea
R atio of LH/FSH > 3:1
I nsulin resistance
A cne
N IDDM risk ↑: at least one-half of women with PCO are obese. Many women with PCO are also hyperinsulinemic and insulin resistant, independent of obesity, compared to normal women.

POST-GASTRECTOMY COMPLICATIONS: "WE B DUMPING FAT !"

W eight loss (due to early satiety and dumping)
E sophagitis, alkaline reflux

B lind loop syndrome—bacterial overgrowth occurs in the afferent loop and causes malabsorption (as bile salts are deconjugated) and megaloblastic anemia as bacteria consume B12.

D umping* (N/V, diarrhea, weakness, abdominal pain, hypoglycemia); Diarrhea*; vit D malabsorption (→ osteomalacia)
U lcerogenic tumors (i.e. gastrinomas)-- Multiple recurrent ulcers, ulcers in unusual places should alert to retained antrum or ulcerogenic tumor.
M arginal ulcer disease (marginal ulcer disease: New ulcerations which occur in the jejunum no more than 2cm distal to anastomosis; usually in efferent loop)
P ernicious anemia (B12 malabsorption due to loss of intrinsic factor)
I ron deficiency anemia
N ausea/vomiting (bilious vomiting*)
G astric stump carcinoma (post-gastrectomy gastric ulcers have a lower incidence of ca than do post-gastrectomy duodenal ulcers)

F olate malabsorption
A fferent loop syndrome (after Billroth II gastroenterostomy; results from partial obstruction of the afferent loop)
T B (reactivation)

*   *Post-vagotomy complications*

COMPLICATIONS OF GASTRECTOMY-- 6 D's: (Remember botulism has 6 D's too!)

D umping
D iarrhea
D izziness
D ysphagia
D eficiencies (vitamins, Fe)
D istension after eating

IMPORTANT POST-SPLENECTOMY INFECTIONS: "Ca.S.H. 'M. Babe !"

C **a**pnocytophaga (DF-2)
S trep Pneumoniae
H Flu

'**M** alaria; <u>M</u>eningitidis, neisseria

B **abe**siosis

Primary Biliary Cirrhosis: PAM'S SICK

P ruritis; <u>P</u>ortal HTN often
A lk phos ↑ (almost always elevated)
M Immunoglobulin Ig <u>M</u> ↑; A<u>M</u>A (anti-<u>m</u>itchondrial antibody) is the serologic hallmark of PBC; <u>M</u>usculoskeletal complaints in at least 40% of patients
S mall bile ducts are the ones affected

S teatorrhea (2° to progressive cholestasis); <u>S</u>kin hyperpigmentation; <u>Sj</u>ogren's symptoms in roughly half the patients
I diopathic disease of middle-aged women
C olchicine & ursodeoxycholic acid (UDCA) important treatment options; <u>C</u>REST syndrome in approximately 10% of patients
K ind of patient with PBC: Consider PBC in those patients , particularly women, who present with the following otherwise-unaccounted-for symptoms: pruritis, fatigue, jaundice, or unexplained weight loss with right upper quadrant discomfort & an ↑ alk phos.

1° <u>HYPER</u>parathyroidism [See Figure 1 (Appendix): <u>ALGORITHMIC</u> <u>APPROACH TO ↑ SERUM CA:</u>]:   ↑ **PTH HARMS**

P TH ↑. If the PTH is ↓, must consider parathyroid-independent hyperCa (tumors; sarcoid; vit D intox; etc); <u>P</u>seudogout.
T reatment is surgery when clinically significant.

H TN; <u>H</u>yperplasia only 15% of the time (e.g. in MEN I, IIA);

H ypercalcemia

A denoma the usual suspect (ie not hyperplasia); adenoma is solitary 80% of the time; usually asymptomatic; Abnormal cognitive function

R enal stones
Rule out: FHH (Familial Hypocalciuric Hypercalcemia), an important differential, since it's a benign disease that precludes surgery. The way to DDx these is by ✓ *Urine Ca. It's low in FHH*; normal to ↑ in 1° hyperpara.

M EN I or IIA might be associated; these types are hyperplastic lesions; Mood (depression) often affected

S keletal lesions that can be found include…periosteal bone resorption e.g. at the distal phalanges → bone fractures; and "Salt and pepper" lesions seen on Skull plain film

PRIMARY PULMONARY HTN

CHEAPEST DRAFTS (or CARPETED SHAFTS *if you like*)

C or pulmonale

H yperreactivity of the pulmonary vasculature

E xertional dyspnea. (In fact, symptoms, in general, are usually related to exertion.)

A ngina

P ulmonary pressures ↑; Prominent pulmonary artery; Pruning of the pulmonary vessels seen on CXR/angiography; Palpitations CXR:

E chocardiography is the most useful imaging modality for confirming pulmonary hypertension. ✓ for TR and ↑MAP The addition of mean right atrial pressure to the peak tricuspid jet velocity gives an accurate noninvasive estimate of peak pulmonary pressure. RV dilatation and RVH are late findings.

S yncope/presyncope

T R murmur

D LCO ↓; Dry cough

R VH, RAD, RAE

A ccentuated P2

F atigue; F>M incidence

T hromboembolism (chronic) ventilation-perfusion lung scanning is a reliable method for differentiating

S $_3$ or S_4 gallops heard over the RV

MANAGEMENT PRINCIPLES IN PPH: **T.A. CODED**

T. ransplantation (lung or heart-lung)
A. nticoagulation for chronic thromboemboli and PPH

C CBs (nifedipine and diltiazem) are first-line therapy.
O xygen for hypoxemia
D iuretics for edema
E poprostenol, PGI_2, prostacyclin (Flolan®) is considered for patients who fail to respond to oral calcium channel blockers
D igoxin for RV failure

PRIMARY SCLEROSING CHOLANGITIS: **PSC CLUES**

P resentation: similar to PBC, with pruritis, fatigue, jaundice, or unexplained weight loss with right upper quadrant discomfort & an ↑ alk phos.
S teatorrhea and fat-soluble vitamin deficiencies (A, D, E, K)
C holangiography (MRCP, ERCP): thickened ducts with multifocal stricturing & dilatation of medium- and large-sized intrahepatic & extrahepatic bile ducts. Cholestatic pattern (similar to PBC) seen on laboratories.

C holangitis a common complication, esp after procedures like endoscopic or surgical manipulation (including liver biopsy) → Ciprofloxacin is employed for prophylaxis & treatment before or after such procedures in PSC patients.   C holangiocarcinoma (↑ risk of bile duct ca); remember too that UC per se also has an ↑ risk of cholangiocarcinoma, i.e. irrespective of PSC). The presentation of cholangiocarcinoma can be indistinguishable with PSC strictures themselves without cytologic brushings of the strictures to exclude malignancy.
L ARGER bile ducts (extra and intrahepatic) suffer an obliterative inflammatory fibrosis
U lcerative Colitis associated in 70% of cases (UC may come before, during, or after the PSC). So all patients initially diagnosed with sclerosing cholangitis should be ruled out for incipient UC.
E levations (asymptomatic) in the alk phos can be an important clue in patients with preexisting UC for the development of PSC.
S tenting of dominant strictures; Supportive treatment, primarily, although many patients require liver transplant

PROGRESSIVE SUPRANUCLEAR PALSY: BANANA PEELS

B radykinesia, rigidity, masked faces and an abnormal gait are all features shared by Parkinson's Disease.

A taxic gait

N o response to levodopa

A xial rigidity

N o tremor

A ge: PSP usually develops after the sixth decade of life

P seudobulbar palsy (spastic weakness of the pharyngeal musculature causing dysphagia, dysarthria, and emotional lability);
Personality change & cognitive dysfunction/dementia
Poor prognosis patients die in a relatively short time from progressive neurologic disease, pneumonias, etc.

E ye movements abnormal → vertical gaze palsy (impaired downward gaze) which leads to…

E arly, frequent falls

L oss of postural reflexes / postural instability → also contributes to falls

S tartled facial expression caused by hypertonicity of the frontalis muscles, occasional retrocollis, and lid retraction.

COMMON CLINICAL SCENARIOS THAT CAN ↑ QT INTERVAL: EPITAPH

E lectrolytes: ↓Mg, ↓K+, ↓Ca;

P entamidine

I schemia: #1 cause; IA antiarrhythmics (e.g. PDQ: procainamide; disopyramide; quinidine)

T ricyclic antidepressants

A miodarone; Any combination of erythromycin/lovastatin /azoles

P henothiazines

H ypothyroidism

PSEUDOMONAS AERUGINOSA: Common Infections & Clinical Settings:

C iN HOT TUBS! (as in you "See (pseudomonas) in hottubs"

C ystic Fibrosis

N ocosomial infections; <u>N</u>eutropenia, esp cellutitis → pyoderma gangrenosum

H ot tubs (→folliculitis); <u>H</u>ospital-aquired infections (nocosomial infections)

O peration; <u>O</u>ptho: contact lens wearers

T rauma, particularly aquatic

T oo much sugar! (DM: malignant otitis externa)

U lcers, chronic decubitus

B urns

S wimmers ear (acute diffuse otitis externa (remember, pseudomonas is a flagellated organism—you're not the only one who likes the water!)

PSEUDOOBSTRUCTION:

MOSES (The Red Sea was only a "pseudoobstruction" to MOSES, who is said to have parted it!)

M echanical obstruction but without occlusion of the lumen; usu. the colon

O gilvie's syndrome = often used to refer to acute intestinal pseudoobstruction

S teatorrhea (caused by bacterial overgrowth)

E sophageal motility abnormal in most patients

S econdary causes include→ amyloidosis, Parkinson's disease, myxedema, hypoparathyroidism, L-Dopa, TCA's, clonidine, phenothiazines, and narcotics.

PULMONARY CAVITATION—COMMON CAUSES: **VIETNAM & S**outh **K**orea

V ascultis (eg PAN, Wegener's)

I nvasive aspergillosis, nocardiosis, actinomycoisis

E mboli

T B (!)

N eoplasms

A BPA, Amebiasis

M ycoses

S trep and Staph pneumonias

K lebsiella

IMPORTANT PUMONARY-RENAL SYNDROMES: **We Go 'Do' Church**

W egener's granulomatosis

G oodpasture's syndrome

D rugs: penicillamine, hydralazine, propylthiouracil (PTU)

C hurg-Strauss syndrome

CONDITIONS ASSOCIATED WITH RAYNAUD'S PHENOMENON:

AMBER's VIB

A rterial diseases

M alignancy (eg ovarian)

B lood disorders (cryoglobulinemia, cold agglutinins, paraproteinemia, polycythemia)

R heumatologic diseases

V asculitides; Vibration injury (!)

I nfections (Parvovirus B19, H. Pylori)

B eta-blockers

REACTIVE ARTHRITIS—GI & GU PRECIPITANTS: Yer. B.U.C.K.S.

Yersinia

B   acteroides
U   reaplasma urealyticum
C   ampylobacter, <u>C</u>hlamydia, <u>C</u>lostridium
K   lebsiella
S   almonella, <u>S</u>higella

REITER'S SYNDROME—KEY FEATURES: C.U.A.C.K.

C   onjunctivitis*
U   rethritis*
A   rthritis*
C   ircinate ballanitis
K   eratoderma blenorrhagicum

  * classic triad

DIAGNOSES TO CONSIDER IN REFRACTORY CHF: ASTHMA COPS

A   sthma; Anemia
S   ilent MI
T   hiamine deficiency
H   igh-ouput failure in elderly (thyrotoxicosis; Paget's dz)
M   yocarditis
A   neurysm, LV

C   ardiac tamponade; <u>C</u>onstrictive pericarditis
O   vervigorous hydration
P   E
S   ilent valvular stenosis

RELAPSING POLYCHONDRITIS—Summary of Key Features: RELAPSING

R espiratory obstruction; Respiratory arrest
E ye findings (episcleritis/scleritis/uveitis)
L aryngeal disease (hoarseness; collapse)
A ssociations: Autoimmune disease in 30%; Aortic insufficiency/Aortic Aneurysm/MVP in 10%; vasculitis in 14%
P olyarthralgias
S wollen, floppy ears (cauliflower appearance)
I nfections, recurrent, due to tracheobronchial degeneration; Increased temp/fever
N asal cartilege inflammation may lead to 'saddle-nose' deformity
G I disease (infrequent)

RENAL DISEASE + JAUNDICE: SHARP *Yellow* BMW

S tauffer syndrome*
H US; Hepatorenal syndrome; Hep B/C; Hantavirus; Hemolysis
A lcohol
R ocky Mountain Spotted Fever (Rickettsia Rickettsiae)
P olycystic Kidney Disease

Y ellow fever

B abesiosis; Brown recluse spider venom
M alaria (2° to massive destruction of RBCs →large amounts of Fe & Hgb overload the liver & kidney)
W eil's disease (leptospirosis)

    * A paraneoplastic, reversible hepatic cellular dysfunction sometimes seen in renal cell carcinoma)

KEY CAUSES OF RENAL ENLARGEMENT: S.C.A.N. H.A.R.D. (*indeed* scan well!)

S arcoidosis; Scleroderma

C ompensatory hypertrophy

A myloidosis

N eoplasm

H ydronephrosis; Hemorrhage; HIV nephropathy

A cute parenchymal disease (nephrotic syndrome, ARF, AIN, pyelo, uric acid nephropathy, acute tubular necrosis

R enal cysts (including Polycystic Kidney Disease); Renal vein thrombosis

D iabetes

RENAL FAILURE & HEMOPTYSIS: "We Go PAINT the CHEST red"

W egener's granulomatosis

G oodpasture's syndrome

P olyarteritis Nodosa (**PAN**)

C ryoglobulinemia

H enoch-Schönlein Purpura (HSP)

E ndocarditis, Emboli

S LE

T B; Thrombosis (renal vein)

✪ RENAL TUBULAR ACIDOSES (RTAs) ✪

	TYPE I	TYPE II	TYPE IV
Location	Distal	Proximal	Distal
Problem	Impaired distal acidification	Reduced proximal bicarb reabsorption	↓ aldo secretion/effect
Serum K+	↓	↓	↑
Urinary pH (5.3 cutoff)	↑	↓	↓
Important examples	Ampho, Sickle cell dz, RA, SLE, Cirrhosis, Lithium	Fanconi's, Amyloidosis, Myeloma, Carbonic anhydrase inhibitors	DM, BPH, NSAIDs, ACEI, Heparin, primary adrenal insuff., CAH, HIV, K+-sparing diuretics, Pentamidine
Management	K+, bicarb	K+, bicarb	Mineralcorticoids, Low K+ diets
Normal Anion Gap Acidosis & Positive Urine Anion Gap (UAG)	✓	✓	✓

✪ **Knowing the urinary pH and the K+ can clinch the diagnosis:**

    ✓   **FIRST** look at the serum K+. If the K+ is ↑, it's Type IV. If not, **THEN** look at the urinary pH ...
    ✓   If the urinary pH is ↑, it's Type I; ↓ is Type II.

Remember also that in **Metabolic Alkalosis...**

✪ a <u>Urine Chloride<10</u> points to <u>surreptious vomiting</u> (loss of HCl yields a met alk)

✪ a <u>Urine Chloride>10</u> points to <u>Bartter's syndrome</u> and <u>diuretics</u>.

MAJOR AND MINOR JONES CRITERIA: SAFER CASES
(must have 2 major or 1major + 2 minor criteria to make the dx)

MINOR

Sore throat
Arthralgias
Fever
EKG changes;↑ **E**SR
Rheumatic History

MAJOR

Carditis
ASO titre↑
Syndenham's chorea
Erythema Marginatum
SQ nodules

PULMONARY INVOLVEMENT IN RHEUMATOID ARTHRITIS: SCRIP CO.

S ubpleural rheumatoid nodules (usually only seen with high titres RF or when additional features are present)

C aplan syndrome (Inflammation and scarring of the lungs in people with rheumatoid arthritis who have exposure to coal dust; aka rheumatoid pneumoconiosis)

R estrictive picture to PFTs and/or ↓DLCO

I nterstitial fibrosis

P leural effusions (re: ↓ glucose, ↓ pH)

C rycoaretenoid joints affected →upper airway obstruction may be seen.

O bliterative bronchiolitis

RHEUMATOLOGIC AUTOANTIBODIES:

➤ **Anti-dsDNA** ☞ **SLE** (70% sensitivity; highly specific); **Anti-ssDNA**→ SLE (100% sensitivity, low specificity)

➤ **Anti-Sm (Smith)** ☞ **SLE** (30% sensitivity but highly specific *if* you see it)

➤ **Anti-RNP** (Ribonuclear protein) ☞ MCTD (**Mixed Connective Tissue Disease**)

➤ Anti-**SS**-A ('anti-Ro') and -B ('anti-La') ☞ **S**jogren's **S**yndrome (also SLE)

➤ **Antihistone protein antibody** ☞ **Drug-induced SLE** (hydralazine and procainamide)

➤ Anti-**Scl**-70 ☞ **Scl**eroderma (Progressive Systemic Sclerosis)

➤ Anti**C**entromere (anti-topoisomerase) ☞ **C**REST

RHINOCEREBRAL MUCORMYCOSIS: **S.N.O.R.E.S. B.A.D.**

S inusitis, acute, is usual presentation with fever, purulent nasal discharge, and sinus pain. All of the sinuses eventually become involved.

N ecrotic lesions around the eyes, nose, and soft and hard palates, or "*eschars*", are hallmark signs of contiguous spread

O pportunistic, fungal infection occurring most often in immunocompromised patients; <u>O</u>verall 25-50% prognosis

R hizopus species are the most common cause of zygomycosis (the other and actually the *preferred* name for mucormycosis*. In any case, these fungi are frequently found on decaying plant and animal products and their spores are present in the air.

E ye swelling (periorbital edema) and eye protrusion (proptosis) and even blindness (if optic nerve is involved) signal contiguous spread to the orbit

S pread of the infection from the sinuses to contiguous structures, such as the palate, orbit and brain, commonly occurs very quickly. Complications therefore can include: **"T.O.N.E. Deaf."**, that's…

> **T** hrombosis of the cavernous sinus
> **O** btundation {following spread of the infection from the ethmoid sinus to the frontal lobe (abscess) }
> **N** erves: cranial nerves II, III, IV, VI, VII, VIII (could do VIII too → tone deaf; but not common)
> **E** ye findings (discussed above)
> **D** eath

B iopsy for confirmation. The hyphae of mucorales are characteristically large, and often twisted or ribbon-like, and are unique among pathogenic fungi in having no septa.

A mpho B + surgical debridement

D KA and/or immunosuppression + mucormycosis → rhinocerebral infections

> * The fungal pathogens that cause mucormycosis belong to the class Zygomycetes and the order Mucorales. *Rhizopus* species are the most commonly isolated agents of mucormycosis followed by *Rhizomucor* species and in fact the genus Mucor only rarely is the cause.

RICKETTSIAL DISEASES* OF MEDICAL IMPORTANCE IN NORTH AMERICA:

RQETSia

R ickettsialpox

Q Fever

E hrlichiosis

T yphus (epidemic, endemic, recrudescent)

S potted fever (Rocky Mt Spotted Fever; actually rickettsialpox also falls under the "spotted fever" serogroup of rickettsial diseases)

* The <u>tick</u> is the vector for Rickettsialpox, RMSF, and Erlichiosis. The human body <u>louse</u> (lice) is the vector for epidemic typhus. The rat <u>flea</u> is the vector for endemic (murine) typhus, and Q fever (coxiella burnetii = organism) has <u>no vector</u>; it's airborne

RISK FACTORS FOR CERVICAL CANCER: LIPSTICK

L ower socioeconomic status

I nfection with HPV (esp high risk subtypes 16, 18)

P oor compliance with appointments (>3y from previous Pap smear)

S TDs (h/o; esp HSV, HIV, HPV)

T obacco use (smoking)

I nvasive or preinvasive disease previously; <u>I</u>mmunosuppression

C ontraceptive hormones

K inky {contact/sex with ≥ 3 partners; early age of first intercourse (<17 yo)}

ROCKY MOUNTAIN SPOTTED FEVER: **ROCKY MT. OYSTERS**

R ickettsia rickettsii is the causative agent

Generally, rickettsiae are obligate intracellular organisms that resemble both a virus and a bacteria. Like bacteria, they have cell walls and are susceptible to antibiotics. Like viruses, they require living cells for growth. They multiply in endothelial cells of small blood vessels and the resulting damage is a "spotted" rash.

Relatively rare in Rocky Mountain states (relative to southeastern and southcentral states)

O nly 60% report a history of a tick bite

C entripetal & centrifugal spread, so-called, ie beginning at ankles/wrists/forearms & spreading outward to the palms/soles and inward to the trunk. Confusion and lethargy are present in 26–28% of cases. Confirmation of clinical diagnosiscan be accomplished with direct immunofluorescent staining of a skin biopsy specimen taken from an area of rash. Serologic confirmation requires acute and convalescent sera to measure a four-fold rise in the titers, or presumptive diagnosis can be made on a single IFA titer of > 1:64. Initiation of therapy should not be delayed for laboratory confirmation.

K idney failure in approx. 20%. (acute renal failure, defined as an elevation in the creatinine above 2 mg/dL). Various mechanisms can contribute to this, including hypotension-induced ATN, intravascular thrombosis, and interstitial vascular inflammation due to direct infection of the endothelial cells by R. rickettsii.

Y oung patients more frequently affected. In the eastern United States, children are infected most frequently. (less than 10 years of age have the highest age-specific incidence of RMSF) In the western United States, disease incidence is highest among adult males.

M ac/pap to petechiae to purpura; Most cases symptomatic between 5 & 7 days after exposure

T ick vectors: Western US → Wood tick = Dermacentor andersoni (tick for Tularemia as well); Eastern US → Dog tick   = Dermacentor variabilis (tick for Tularemia & Erlichiosis as well); Thrombocytopenia from increased destruction at sites of rickettsia-mediated vascular injury

O ther symptoms frequently associated with RMSF include myalgias, nausea or vomiting, abdominal pain

<u>O</u>nly about 50% of patients presenting on or before the 3rd day of illness have the classic triad of fever, rash, headache; therefore…

Y ou must treat empirically if the historical and clinical features suggest a diagnosis of RMSF; ie you don't have to have the rash. Delay of appropriate antibiotics beyond the 4 th day of illness significantly contributes to mortality.

S erum sodium commonly ↓

T reatment: Doxycycline is by far the commonly used; chloramphenicol for pregnant women; antibiotics should be continued up to 5-7 days after resolution of the fever; <u>T</u>ransaminitis with ↑ AST frequently seen

E xtensive cutaneous necrosis due to DIC occurs in 4%; these may become gangrenous)

R ash on 4th day of fever (range 2-6 days); sudden onset F/C, severe H/A; rash may be absent in up to 13% of cases (so-called "spotless RMSF")

S pring and early summer, when outdoor activity is most frequent

<u>S</u>outheastern and south-central states are the 2 most endemic regions. North Carolina and Oklahoma account for one third of cases. South Carolina, Tennessee, and Georgia represent the third, fourth, and fifth biggest states for RMSF. Less than 2% of the total number of cases are found in the Rocky Mountain states.

ROSACEA: **CATSUP**

C apillary hypersensitivity to various aggravating or exacerbating factors, including: sun exposure, emotional stress, hot or cold weather, alcohol, spicy foods (catsup is a poor substitute for salsa), hot beverages, exercise, & certain skin products leading to flushing and ultimately to telangiectasias; <u>C</u>entral face predominantly affected; <u>C</u>eltic peoples and southern Italians; <u>C</u>hronic, relapsing disorder

A cneiform disorder of the facial pilosebaceous units. Previously called acne rosacea but is unrelated to acne (though frequently coexists); <u>A</u>voidance of any recognizable aggravating factors is, of coure, important.

T reatment: topical metronidazole (or clinda if pregnant) is first-line; if these fail or for more severe dz, PO TCN or minocycline; if still those fail, then oral or topical retinoid therapy is an option. Oral tetracycline and doxycycline effectively control the ocular symptoms of rosacea. Laser treatment is an option for progressive telangiectasis or rhinophyma.

S tages, four: (1) facial flushing, (2) erythema and/or edema and ocular symptoms (eg conjunctivitis/blepharitis), (3) papules and pustules, and (4) rhinophyma.
U nlike acne vulgaris, no comedones (whiteheads)
P eak incidence between 40-50 yo

COMMON AGGRAVATING FACTORS CAN TEASE OUT ROSACEA:

T emp: sun exposure; hot or cold weather; hot baths, hot drinks, "hot" (spicy) foods
E motion
A lcohol
S kin-care products, Spicy foods
E xercise

INDICATIONS FOR STEROIDS IN SARCOIDOSIS: P.H.O.N.I.C.S.

P rogressive pulmonary disease
H ypercalcemia
O cular involvement (eg uveitis)
N eurologic involvement
I nsufficiency (renal) with hypercalciuria
C ardiac involvement
S kin manifestations (disfiguring); eg lupus pernio-violaceous nodules occurring over the nose and malar regions)

KEY FEATURES OF SARCOIDOSIS: OBSCENE FACE
(also a reminder that CN VII often affected)

O cular involvement: eg blurred vision, uveitis
B ilateral hilar adenopathy; Big liver
S ystemic disease involving non-caseating granulomas throughout the body
C alcium ↑ in serum & urine
E nodosum
N onproductive Cough; Dyspnea
Neuro involvement: eg cranial nerve palsies, esp facial, and meningeal involvement
E tiology unknown

F alse-negative PPD (2° to suppressed T lymphocyte function)
A CE levels are non-specific and are corroborative only.
Arthralgias
C ardiac involvement: dysrhythmias, cardiomyopathy
Common presentation on the boards: black women (B>W, M>F) in her 20's-30's with bilateral hilar LN +, E. nodosum/uveitis/dry cough ± hypercalcemia
E ctopic vitamin D

SPONTANEOUS BACTERIAL PERITONITIS (SBP):   FAT SBP

F ever
A scites; Abdominal pain; Altered mental status
T hird generation cephalosporin for ≥ 5 days for mgmt

S ingle organism—nearly always; Enterobacteriaceae #1; Strep pneumo #2; enterococci #3
B elly tender; Bedside inoculation of ascitic fluid into blood culture bottles dramatically increases the culture positive sensitivity since SBP is a low-colony-count monomicrobial infection similar to bacteremia; ↓ BP (20% of patients at time of dx)
P MNs (neutrophils) > 250/mm3 (or WBC > 500) = important cell counts to know since often culture negative (see "B" above); Paralytic ileus

SCHISTOCYTES—Important Causes of Microangiopathic Hemolytic Anemia:

SAD PATH

S LE
A cute glomerulonephritis
D IC

P AN; Pulmonary hypertension
A cute renal failure
T TP
H US; HTN (malignant); HELLP (hemolysis, elevated liver enzymes, low platelets in pregnancy)

SCLERODERMA—KEY FEATURES: G.I. W.A.R.D.S.

G ERD/Heartburn
I nterstitial pulmonary fibrosis → elevated pulmonary pressure (pulmonary hypertension)

W eight Loss, Weakness/fatigue
A rthralgias/myalgias
R enal crisis (treat with an ACE inhibitor), Raynaud's phenomenon
D ysphagia, Dyspnea, ↓ DLCO (related to "I" above); Digital ulceration, gangrene
S tricture formation, Stiffness (joints)

SCROTAL MASSES: HE VOMITS

H ydrocoele; Hematocoele
E pididymitis, Epididymal cyst

V aricocoele
O rchitis
M alignancy
I ndirect inguinal hernia
T orsion
S permatocoele

IMPORTANT CAUSES OF SECONDARY HYPERLIPIDEMIA: D.E.L. N.A.C.H.O.S.!

D iabetes
E strogen therapy
L iver disease (hepatic)

N ephrotic syndrome
A lcoholism
C hronic renal failure
H ypothyroidism
O besity
S ustenance/sad diet → del nachos!

IMPORTANT COMMON CAUSES OF SECONDARY THROMBOCYTOSIS:

"I.'M. H.O.T." (also helps you recall inflammation/infection below)

I nfection (acute); Inflammation (chronic inflammatory conditions, eg RA, IBD, TB, sarcoidosis, Wegener's granulomatosis); Iron deficiency anemia
M yeloproliferative disorders (P. Vera, CML)

H emorrhage, Hemolysis
O peration (post-splenectomy)
T umor

SEMinomas are highly radio**SEN**sitive, and only 10% secrete <u>Beta-HCG</u>; never AFP!!

NON-seminomas on the other hand do not respond to XRT and secrete <u>both</u>
<u>AFP and Beta-HCG</u>. This is clearly summarized in the following table:

	SEMINOMA	NON-SEMINOMA
AFP	**<u>No</u>**	Yes
B-HCG	Yes	Yes

SERONEGATIVE SPONDYLOARTHROPATHIES: REAP

R eiter's/<u>R</u>eactive arthritis
E nteropathic arthritis
A nkylosing spondylitis
P soriatic arthritis

SEROTONIN SYNDROME—CLINICAL FEATURES: MISMATCH *

M yoclonus
I rritability, <u>I</u>ncoordination
S hivering
M ental status changes
A gitation
T remor
C onfusion
H yperreflexia

SEROTONIN SYNDROME: *Coadministration of an SSRI with any of the*
following drugs can result in: → a serotonin **SANDBLAST ! ...**

S umatriptan
A mphetamines
N arcotics (cocaine, meperidine)
D HE

B uspirone
L ithium
A ntidepressants: MAO inhibitors, nefazodone, trazodone anorexants
      (fenfluramine)
S elegiline
T ricyclic antidepressants

SERUM SICKNESS: Drugs' F.A.U.L.T.

Seen 5-14 days after initial exposure to the drug or 2-4 days after subsequent exposure

D rugs (the most common cause of serum sickness is PCN)

F ever

A rthralgias; Adenopathy

U rticarial rash; less commonly may see a morbilliform or scarlatiniform rash; palpable purpura; erythema simplex or multiforme

L ymphadenopathy

T ype III hypersensitivity reaction with immune complex disease, or classic arthrus reaction

IMPORTANT CAUSES OF SERUM SICKNESS: "B.A.D. A.S.S."

B arbiturates (in addition to the ANTI-drugs below); Hepatitis B

A ntitoxins or antivenoms derived from horse serum; examples include products for preventing or treating snakebites (antivenom is a classic example), botulism, tetanus, and rabies; Antithymocyte globulin (ATG) is another.

D rugs: esp. the ANTI-Drugs! If you can comfortably put an "Anti" in front of the drug category, it probably fits here! :

Antibiotics	→ eg, PCN, cephalosporins, ciprofloxacin, tetracyclines, griseofulvin, itraconazole, metronidazole, rifampicin, streptomycin, sulfanilamides
Antiarrhythmics	→ eg procainamide, quinidine
Antidepressants	→ eg fluoxetine, bupropion
Antiepileptics	→ eg phenytoin, carbamazepine
Antiinflammatories	→ eg naproxen, sulindac, Indomethacin, penicillamine
Antihypertensives	→ eg propranolol, captopril, methyldopa, hydralazine

A llopurinol (in addition to the ANTI-drugs above)

S treptokinase.

S tings from insects of the order Hymenoptera (eg, bees, mosquitoes)

IMPORTANT CAUSES OF SIADH: Pituitary **ADENOMA**

P ulmonary diseases, particularly pneumonias, but also COPD, pulmonary abscess, TB; Pain

A ny CNS disorder, including (posterior "pituitary adenoma"), stroke, hemorrhage, infection, trauma, encephalitis, meningitis, and psychosis can enhance ADH release.

D rugs—see DOLPHINS mnemonic below

E ctopic ADH production (oat cell lung ca)

N ausea

O ther (idiopathic)

M ajor abdominal or thoracic surgery

A IDS

SIADH-inducing Drugs: TOBASCO

T hiazide diuretics

O xytocin

B arbiturates; Bromocryptine

A ntipsychotics (thiothixene, thioridazine, haloperidol, Chlorpromazine); Amphetamine derivative ecstasy (MDMA); Analgesics (NSAIDs, opiates)

S SRIs; Sertraline

C arbamazepine; Chlorpropamide; Cyclophosphamide; Clofibrate; Cytotoxics (vincristine; vinblastine; cysplatin)

O thers: amitriptylline; sertraline; MAO inhibitors

SIADH-IMPORTANT CAUSES: DOLPHINS
(salt water mammal, so you remember high urine Na+!)

D rugs

O at cell (small cell) lung carcinoma

L ung diseases, other: COPD, pneumonia, TB, abscess

P ain

H ead trauma, CVA, meningitis

I nfection, esp HIV

N ausea

S urgery (major), Steroids ↓ (corticosteroids)

SICKLE CELL COMPLICATIONS: "G.A.R.L.I.C makes me Sick As Hell" (Sickle Cell) :

G allstone formation due to excessive bilirubin production
A septic necrosis (Avascular necrosis)
R enal: focal segmental glomerulonephropathy; papillary necrosis;
L eg ulcers, chronic
I nfections (eg pneumococcal, salmonella), including osteomyelitis
C rises; Cerebrovascular complications (eg CVA)

MAIN TYPES OF SICKLE CELL CRISES: **M.I.S.H.A.P.**

M egaloblastic
I nfarctive (aka "vasoocclusive" or "painful"; eg priapism and Acute Chest Syndrome[1])
S equestration[2]
H emolytic
A plastic[3]
P ulmonary crisis (aka Acute chest syndrome *; may be considered a form of infarctive crisis)

1. Fast or difficult breathing may indicate an *Acute Chest Syndrome* (ACS) -- that is, pulmonary involvement secondary to lung infarct or infection, alone, or in combination. This pulmonary crisis causes 20% of SS deaths. Look for Fever, tachypnea, leukocytosis, chest pain, and pulmonary infarcts. In adults, sickling here is usually unaccompanied by infection.

2. The sudden entrapment of a large portion of the blood volume in the spleen leads to findings of pallor, splenomegaly, and worsening anemia and when severe, signs of cardiovascular collapse due to the accompanying acute blood loss. Labs show anemia, ↑ retic count; ↓ platelets.

3. An *aplastic crisis*, precipitated by a temporary arrest of red cell production in the bone marrow, is usually caused by parvovirus infection. Pallor, fatigue, or decreased activity are the principal signs and symptoms. A blood count reveals a fall in the hemoglobin and hematocrit levels and reticulocytopenia.

RHEUMATOLOGIC MANIFESTATIONS OF SICKLE CELL DISEASE:

SHAG!—*"Yeah Baby!"*

S ickle crisis (lower extremity arthralgias (usually knees, ankles); myalgias; synovitis; <u>S</u>eptic arthritis (osteomyelitis; esp <u>S</u>almonella, particularly if hyposplenic)

H emochromatotic arthropathy 2° to iron overload due to frequent transfusions

A vascular (aka 'Aseptic') necrosis

G out

SOMATOSTATINOMA (*delta cells of the <u>pancreas</u> overproduce somatostatin*)

$\underline{S}^3$

S teatorrhea

S tones (cholelithiasis)

S ugar (diabetes)

<u>SOMOGYI EFFECT vs. DAWN PHENOMENON:</u>   *<u>PEARL</u>:*

✪ ***SOMOGYI** effect* = ***rebound hyperglycemia*** <u>**2° to release of**</u> <u>counter-regulatory hormones</u> that follow a hypoglycemic episode (these hypoglycemic episodes are often accompanied by <u>vivid nightmares</u>)

> ***TREATMENT*** → 1) Take the NPH or lente insulin before bed. Instead of before dinner; or 2) switch to a longer-acting insulin preparation (such as ultralente insulin).

✪ ***DAWN** phenomenon* = ↑ early AM glusoses <u>**2° to insulin resistance**</u> (there is an increased need for insulin in the early morning due to the early morning release of growth hormone which antagonizes the action of insulin.)

> ***TREATMENT*** → increase the patient's insulin.

<u>**NOTE**</u>*: Both of these early AM phenomena are hyperglycemic in nature, yet the treatments are exact opposites. Usually the dawn phenomenon can be differentiated from posthypoglycemic hyperglycemia (Somogyi) by* <u>**measuring the blood glucose at 3 AM**</u> *(↓ in Somogyi).*

SPUR CELLS & BURR CELLS—WHICH IS WHICH?

➤ <u>Spur</u> cells (Acanthocytes) → <u>liver</u> disease; *WHEREAS*…

➤ <u>Burr</u> cells→<u>Uremia</u>; if you confuse spur and burr cells, you may choose to recall that in advanced uremia, the concentration of urea in sweat may be so high that, after evaporation, a fine white powder can be found on the skin surface, so-called "<u>uremic frost</u>", so burr goes with uremia!

ST DEPRESSION—CAUSES: MED SLIP (when you slip, you fall *down*)

M VP

E mbolism (PE)

D ilated cardiomyopathy, <u>D</u>igoxin toxicity (also quinidine)

S ubendocardial ischemia or infarct, <u>S</u>hock

L V enlargement with strain

I nferior wall MI reciprocal ST depression, <u>I</u>ntracranial hemorrhage

P otassium loss

CAUSES OF AN ST ELEVATION: PHALLIC pole

P ericarditis (diffuse, concave ST ↑; PR depression often noted)

H yperkalemia

A neurysm, ventricular

L VH

L BBB

I schemia

C oronary spasm (Prinztmetal's angina); <u>C</u>HF

+ Early re**pol**arization

STATISTICS: SENSITIVITY, SPECIFICITY, & PREDICTIVE VALUES an *EASIER* way:

ALWAYS SET UP YOUR 2X2 TABLE THIS WAY:

	DISEASE PRESENT	DISEASE ABSENT
DIAGNOSTIC TEST +	True + "a"	False + "b"
DIAGNOSTIC TEST -	False - "c"	True - "d"

IMPORTANT NOTES:

- ✪ *Don't put the headings on the wrong axis !!*
- ✪ **The most important players are "a" and "d"**—remember their positions!
- ✪ **Sensitivity** goes **down the 1st column**!
- ✪ **Specificity** goes **down the 2nd column**!
- ✪ **Positive Predictive Value (PPV)** goes **across the 1st row**!
- ✪ **Negative Predictive Value (NPV)** goes **across the 2nd row**!

SO, setting up again spatially much simpler this time, it goes like this:
{CAPS MEANS ALWAYS ON TOP, except for prevalence}

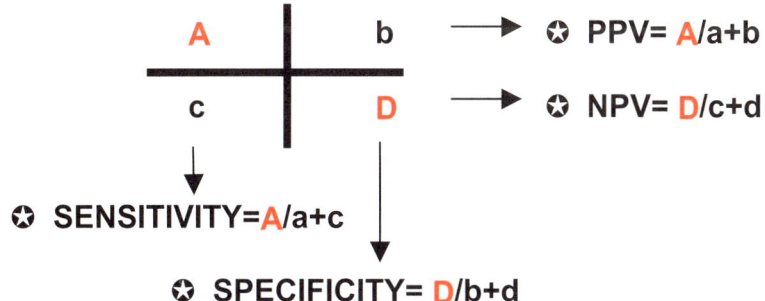

✪ PPV= A/a+b

✪ NPV= D/c+d

✪ SENSITIVITY=A/a+c

✪ SPECIFICITY= D/b+d

✪ And PREVALENCE= a+c/a+b+c+d

STEATOHEPATITIS (FATTY LIVER)—CAUSES: SPORTS ADDICT

S   tarvation, protein-calorie malnutrition, rapid weight loss
P   regnancy
O   besity
R   eye's syndrome
T   PN
S   ilent 's'! (nothing here)

A   lcohol
D   iabetes
D   rugs—esp corticosteroids, TCN, valproic acid, ketoprofen, amiodarone, MDMA (ecstasy), didanosine (ddI), stavudine, synthetic estrogens, calcium channel blockers, tamoxifen, methotrexate, cocaine)
I   BD, Infection with HIV
C   ushing's syndrome (includes obesity and corticosteroids here)
T   hyrotoxicosis

STERILE PYRURIA—CAUSES OF: TRACT

T   B
R   eiter's syndrome
A   nalgesic nephropathy
C   hlamydia, Chronic interstitial cystitis, Calculi (persistent inflammation)
T   RACT infection (UTI inadequately treated); Tumor

STILL'S DISEASE: RASH

R   ash, salmon-colored
A   rthralgias, Antineutrophil antibodies
S   plenomegaly
H   igh white count and temp

The **triad** of Still's however, is the **F**ever, the **A**rthritis, and the **R**ash (**FAR**). Perhaps → "Board *scores* are **STILL FAR** away"

✪ Remember, Strep A **throat AND skin** infections can both lead to post-streptococcal glomerulonephritis.

STREPTOCOCKUS—IMPORTANT INFECTIONS: PENILE SUPPORTS

P haryngitis
E rysipelas
N ecrotizing fasciitis
I mpetigo
L ymphangitis
E ndocarditis

S carlet fever
U TIs
P neumonia
P ost-streptoccal GN
O titis
R heumatic fever
T oxic shock syndrome
S inusitis

STRESS ULCERS: Curling's vs. Cushing's:

- ✓ Cushing's and Curling's ulcers
- ✓ **Curling's ulcers** follow **_burns_** (might think: Curling iron)
- ✓ **Cushing's ulcers** are seen in 50-75 % of **_head injuries_** (might remember: the injury could have been prevented had they been wearing their helmet, or "cushion")

- ✓ Bleeding occurs in 10-20% from 3-7 days following the stress (trauma, stress, illness, burns, etc) if no prophylactic regimen is instituted (Sucralfate; H_2 blockers)

SUDDEN INCREASE IN ASCITES IN PREVIOUSLY STABLE CIRRHOSIS:

HASHISH (can also give you a big belly!)

H epatic vein thrombosis (Budd-Chiari syndrome)
A lcohol binge
S BP (esp if fever/chills/abdominal pain)
H epatorenal syndrome
I ntestinal (UGI) hemorrhage
S epsis
H epatoma (hepatocellular carcinoma); ✓ alpha fetoprotein; re: Hep B and carry an ↑ risk of cirrhosis→hepatoma; Hep A does not.

SUDDEN RESPIRATORY ARREST: SPACE (as in "Give him space!")

S udden obstruction

P neumothorax

A sthma

C HF, <u>C</u>ardiac causes (MI, Tamponade, arrhythmias)

E mbolus, pulmonary

SWEET'S SYNDROME: "D.A.N.A.'S. F.A.T." (*from eating too much Sweet's!*)

D ense dermal infiltrate of neutrophils on biopsy

A ka "Acute Febrile Neutrophilic Dermatosis"

N eutrophilia

A ssociation with <u>A</u>ML and febrile URIs

S teroids yield a prompt response

F ever

A rthralgia

T ender, red plaques to face, upper trunk, extremities

CAUSES OF TALL R-WAVE (R>S) IN V1 OR V2: "WARN HIM DR !"

W PW→ ✓ for delta wave, short PR, and pseudoinfarction pattern ('Q-waves')

A xis deviation to the right

R otation of heart (5% of population)

N ormal variant among young females

H ypertrophic cardiomyopathy

I nfarction, posterior wall

M isplaced leads

D extrocardia

R BBB; RVH

SYSTEMIC MASTOCYTOSIS: **GET UP!**

G I symptoms (eg N/V; abdom pain; PUD; diarrhea; GI bleeding) in 50% of patients

E xcess mast cells in numerous organs, most notably: bone marrow, liver, spleen, lymph nodes, gastrointestinal tract, bones, and skin[1]

T ryptase levels (serum) to differentiate SM from anaphylaxis. SM is strongly suspected in patients with baseline levels of total tryptases of greater than 20 ng/mL and with a ratio of greater than 20 between total tryptase and beta tryptase (yes, that's 20-20!)

U rticaria pigmentosa[2] (UP) = classic rash of SM; the most common manifestation of mastocytosis; basically cutaneous mastocytosis
Urinary histamine levels ↑ (24h specimen). The ↑ histamine levels reflect the release of mast cell mediators due to a greater mast cell burden and can result in flushing & diarrhea (as well as vasodilation, hypotension, pruritus, syncope, fatigue, headache). A urinary histamine concentration of up to 30 ng/mL is considered normal. Levels of histamine are elevated in adults with systemic mastocytosis, but not in those with skin-limited disease.

P ruritis (bath pruritis; similar to P. Vera);
Prognosis: generally excellent. However, the disappearance of UP in patients who initially present with skin lesions portends a poor prognosis.

1   Cutaneous mast cell accumulations can be identified by Darier's sign, which is the finding of urticaria and erythema on rubbing/scratching/ stroking affected skin.

2   Pruritus associated with UP is commonly exacerbated by changes in temperature, local friction (see previous footnote), as well as ingestion of spicy food, hot beverages, ethanol and certain drugs.

TERATOGENIC DRUGS: **FEW MORTALS**

F luorouracil, Finasteride
E pileptic drugs: phenytoin, valproate, carbamazepine
W arfarin

M isoprostol, Metronidazole, Methotrexate
O ral contraceptives
R etinoids (eg acitretin, isotretinoin)
T halidomide, Tetracycline
A ndrogens, ACE inhibitors, ASA
L ithium
S teroids, Streptomycin

THEOPHYLLINE dose should be monitored especially closely when used in:
(all of the following slow the rate of elimination of theo): **COOLS** down

C HF; COPD
O besity
O ral contraceptives
L iver disease (severe)
S imultaneous use of these drugs can ↑ theo levels: **FACED COP**:

F luoroquinolones (e.g. cipro)
A llopurinol
C imetidine
E rythromycin
D igoxin

C CBs (verapamil; diltiazem)
O ral contraceptives
P ropranolol

THRYOID NODULES—90% Rule Of Thumb:

☞ 90% are benign
☞ 90% (!) are "cold" (Note: only 20% of these are actually malignant;
  1% for hot nodules)
☞ 90% are solid

METABOLIC SIDE EFFECTS OF THIAZIDE DIURETICS:

What labs go <u>up</u>?   G.L.U.

- H   yper**G**lycemia (<u>GLU</u>cose)
- H   yper**L**ipidemia
- H   yper**U**ricemia

What labs go <u>down</u>?   P.M.S. (Feeling down?)

- L   ow **P**otassium
- L   ow **M**agnesium
- L   ow **S**odium

3 BASIC PROCESSES THAT GIVE THROMBOCYTOPENIA:

➢ **Decreased production** (check for *megakaryocytes** on peripheral smear or bone marrow; analogous to checking reticulocyte count in anemia)
➢ **Increased destruction** (analogous to hemolysis in anemia)
➢ **Splenic sequestration**

   *   Once you've ruled out decreased production, consider these as
       common causes of platelet destruction or consumption:
       <u>SIT *Down*</u>: **S**plenomegaly, **I**TP, **T**TP, **D**IC

U.S. <u>TICK-BORNE DISEASES</u> ON THE BOARDS: B ALERT !

- **B**   **A**besiosis
- **L**   yme disease
- **E**   rlichiosis
- **R**   ocky Mt Spotted Fever; <u>R</u>elapsing Fever
- **T**   ularemia; <u>T</u>ick paralysis

✓ All of these have tick vectors, and each of these shares tick vectors with ≥1 of the other diseases. (*See Venn diagram on this*).

✓ *Other* US Tick-borne diseases include:
  ▪ Colorado Tick Fever, Coxiella Burnetti (the causative organism in Q Fever)
  ▪ Relapsing Fever—Borrelia spirochetes (can be tick- or louse-borne)

"OVERBITES", i.e. OVERLAPPING TICK BITES: WHICH TICKS ARE RESPONSIBLE FOR WHICH DISEASES?

DISEASE	TICK	COMMON TICK NAME
BABESIOSIS	Ixodes Scapularis (aka Ixodes Dammini)	Black-legged tick (aka Deer tick)
LYME DISEASE	Ixodes Scapularis; I. Pacificus	Black-legged tick (aka Deer tick)
ERLICHIOSIS	*Human Monocytic Erlichiosis (HME):* Dermacentor variabilis; Amblyomma americanum; *Human Granulocytic Erlich*iosis *(HGE):* Ixodes Scapularis	American dog tick; Lonestar tick Black-legged tick (aka Deer tick)
ROCKY MT SPOTTED FEVER	Dermacentor variabilis; Dermacentor andersoni	American dog tick; Rocky Mt wood tick
TULAREMIA	Dermacentor variabilis; Dermacentor andersoni; Amblyomma americanum	American dog tick; Rocky Mt wood tick; Lonestar tick

VENN DIAGRAM ILLUSTRATING THE SHARED RELATIONSHIPS BETWEEN TICK VECTORS & KEY DISEASES TO KNOW:

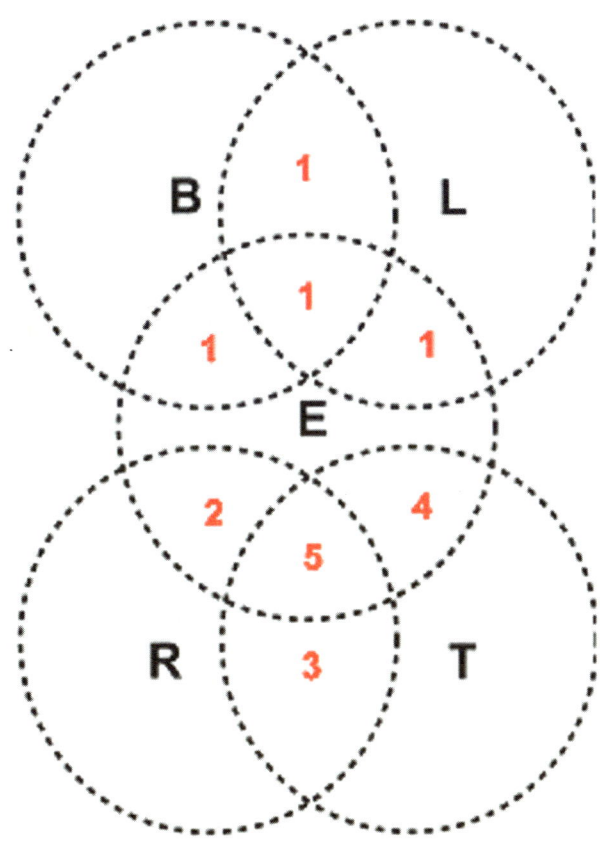

LEGENDS:

B = Babesiosis
L = Lyme Disease
E = Erlichiosis
R = Rocky Mt Spotted Fever
T = Tularemia

B/L/E = Ixodes Scapularis[1] (blacklegged tick, or "deer tick")

R/E =   Dermacentor Variabilis[2]

R/T =   Dermacentor Andersoni[3]

E/T =   Amblyomma Americanum[4]

R/E/T = Dermacentor Variabilis[5]

TORSADES DE POINTES—Drugs Causing: "Mama Always Prays Friday 13th!"

M ycins (erythromycins, etc)

A zoles (ketoconazole; itraconazole; sulfamethoxazole)

P entamidine; Psychotropics (eg phenothiazines; SSRIs; respiridone; TCAs; haloperidol)

F luoroquinolones

I A (class IA antiarrhythmics: Procainamide; Disopyramide; Quinidine)

III (class III antiarrhythmics: Bretylium; Amiodarone; Sotalol; Ibutilide)

TOXIGENIC BACTERIAL DIARRHEAS (watery; no fecal leukocytes):

CAVE B (B for Binladen or just B for Burial !)

C lostridium (C. **P**erfringens[1]; C. diff.; C. botulinum)

A ureus, **S**taph[1]

V ibrio cholerae; Vibrio parahemolyticus

E nterotoxigenic E. Coli (ETEC)

B acillus[1] cereus

> [1] Single underline = "**PBS**" = **P**reformed **B**acterial **S**ystem of endotoxins in ingested food (*food poisoning*).
> The rest = infectious gastroenteritis caused by enterotoxin-producing bacteria

TTP (Thrombotic Thrombocytopenic Purpura): F.A.T. R.N.

F ever

A nemia (microangiopathic hemolytic anemia); hemolysis→ *schistocytes*

T hrombocytopenia

R enal findings

N eurologic findings

... **HUS (HEMOLYTIC UREMIC SYNDROME)**

is **SIMILAR** to TTP, **except without** the Fever or Neurologic involvement (i.e. "F**AT R**N" without the 'F' or the 'N'):

F ever—not typical for HUS
A nemia—microangiopathic hemolytic
T hrombocytopenia

R enal insufficiency
N eurologic complications—not typical for HUS

TULAREMIA: **LUST 4 FACTS**

L iver enzymes abnormal in approximately 50 % of patients.
U lceroglandular disease accounts for 60 to 80 % of cases & manifests as fever and a single erythematous papuloulcerative lesion with a central eschar. {Other clinical syndromes far less common (GUT POO: (Glandular Ulceroglandular Typhoidal Pneumonic Oculoglandular Oropharyngeal)}
S erology can confirm diagnosis at 2 weeks—usually via tube agglutination or ELISA.
T icks & Rabbits are important vectors. Suspect tularemia in cases involving rabbits/rabbit hunting—in fact tularemia is sometimes called "rabbit fever"),

4

F rancisella tularensis is a small, facultative gram-negative intracellular coccobacillus, and causes this zoonosis
A brupt onset of fever, chills, headache, and malaise, after an incubation period of 2 to 10 days.
C ontracted via the skin, gut (ingestion) and pulmonary routes.
- Skin - through a cut in the skin when handling infected animals, or being bitten by an infected deer fly or tick, is the most common way of getting tularemia.
- Stomach - by eating contaminated wild meat (e.g. rabbit) that has not been sufficiently cooked, or less commonly by drinking contaminated, untreated water.
- Lungs - the bacteria can be inhaled by breathing in dust from contaminated soil.
T ender regional lymphadenopathy typically accompanies the ulceroglandular skin lesion
S treptomycin is the drug of choice

TUMOR LYSIS SYNDROME: KEY LABS: (don't confuse this section with a similar looking section (earlier), called "Metabolic Side Effects Of Thiazide Diuretics")

What goes up?   **BuLK UP !**

BUN
L DH
K + ↑
U ric acid ↑
P hosphate ↑

What goes down?   **A.B.C.D**.ecrease!

Acidosis (pH ↓)
Bicarbonate
Calcium; **C**reatinine clearance

TURNER'S SYNDROME: FeMaLe SHOWCASES

F emale phenotype
e
M icrognathia (small jaw); Miscarriages ↑ (in up to 50%)
a
L ow-set ears; Low hairline
e

S treak gonads (lack both germ cells and hormone-producing cells)
H ypothyroid (20-30%)
O ne of the two X chromosomes is either missing or abnormal
W ebbed neck
C arrying angle at the elbows is ↑
Coarctation + Aortic Stenosis = Noonan's syndrome
Cleft, high palate
Congenital heart malformations (20-30%): coarctation; bicuspid AV; MVP
A menorrhea—in fact this is the #1 cause of 1° amenorrhea
S hield-like chest
E picanthal folds
S hort stature; Short 4th metacarpals/metatarsals

T-WAVE INVERSIONS—CAUSES OF: **DUBLIN** **P**ub ('bottoms up?" → T-wave inversions!)

D igoxin; Dilated (and hypertrophic) cardiomyopathies
U nstable angina
B undle Branch Blocks
L VH
I schemia; Infarction; Idiopathic
N ormal (esp young, black), Neuro (CVA)

P ericarditis, Prolapse (MVP), Paced beats (ventricular)

TYPE IV RTA "vs." BARTTER'S SYNDROME

It might help you to remember one if you know the other since they are practically *opposites* in these regards:

	TYPE 4 RTA	BARTTER'S Syndrome
Renin	↓	↑
Aldo	↓	↑
K+	↑	↓
BP	↑	↓/normal
Acid-base	Met. **acidosis** (nonAG)	Met. **Alkalosis** (Chloride-resistant)

RESPONSE OF COMPLICATIONS OF ULCERATIVE COLITIS TO <u>COLECTOMY</u>:

1. ***P**ositive* Response

   a. **P** eripheral arthropathy (don't confuse with hemochromatosis, where treatment *does not* improve the arthropathy)
   b. **P** yoderma gangrenosum (and the other noteworthy dermatologic manifestation, erythema nodosum)
   c. **P** ara-rectal disease

2. ***Unresponsive (**S**tays the **S**ame)***

   a. **S** pondilitis, ankylosing
   b. **S** clerosing cholangitis

MANAGEMENT IN UNSTABLE ANGINA: PAGAN, B.C.

P TCA
A SA + heparin
G lycoprotein IIb, IIIa inhibitors
A ntiplatelet agents, other: eg clopidogrel, ticlodipine
N itroglycerin

B eta-blockers
C ABG

MANAGEMENT OF UNSTABLE ANGINA (in greater detail):   CIGAR

C atheterization (Emergent catheterization is performed for prolonged episodes of angina unresponsive to medical therapy or for frequent recurrent episodes of ischemic chest pain.)

I ntravenous nitroglycerin; Intravenous beta blocker are given as <u>antiischemic therapy</u> for symptom control: metoprolol, propranolol, and esmolol are the ones that have been studied the most.

G lycoprotein IIb/IIIa inhibitors in high risk patients unstable angina patients, defined by the ACC/AHA Task Force and the Sixth American College of Chest Physicians (ACCP) Consensus Conference on Antithrombotic Therapy as those who: 1) manifest continuing ischemia or 2) have other high-risk features; and 3) to patients in whom a percutaneous coronary intervention is planned. Generally speaking, though, glycoprotein IIb/IIIa inhibitors are not given to low risk UA patients (no $\uparrow$ in cardiac enzymes; no ST$\downarrow$, chest pain resolved) or patients with no prior angina; no ergional or global LVD; and no perfusion defects.

A spirin (*Clopidogrel or ticlopidine* can be given to patients who cannot take aspirin because of gastrointestinal intolerance or hypersensitivity.) <u>+ heparin</u> (given by intravenous infusion, not subcutaneous or intravenous bolus) reduces progression to MI and perhaps mortality . *Low molecular weight heparin* is an alternative to heparin; it has at least equivalent efficacy, and is easier to administer and has a lower incidence of thrombocytopenia.

R evascularization ($\pm$) (Patients who are considered high risk who undergo revascularization should be considered for early angiography within the first 24 to 36 hours. Remember, as many as 15 % of such patients have no significant coronary stenosis on angiography. Some of these patients may have coronary microvascular disease.)

UPPER LOBE INFILTRATES—IMPORTANT CAUSES: TRASH

T B

R adiation fibrosis (& another Fibrosis—CF)

A nkylosing spondylitis; Aspergillosis

S ilicosis; Sarcoidosis

H istiocytosis X

WHEN TO USE URICOSURIC AGENTS (eg Probenicid):   4N

N o history of renal stone formation

N ot overproducing uric acid

N ot over 60 yo

N ormal renal function

DRUGS WHICH CAN CAUSE URINARY INCONTINENCE: ABCD'S

A lcohol

    Alpha-blockers

    Alpha agonists

    Anticholinergics

    Antidepressants

    Antipsychotics

    Analgesic narcotics

B eta-blockers

C alcium channel blockers

D iuretics

S edative-hypnotics

VALPROATE—SIDE EFFECTS: **Pee → WETLANDS ***

P olyuria */Polydipsia*; Pancreatitis

W eight gain

E dema *

T remor; Thrombocytopenia

L iver toxicity; Lethargy; Leukopenia

A lopecia; Appetite increased

N ausea and/or vomiting *

D iabetes insipidus*; Dizziness; Drowsiness;

S ensitivity to light

VENTRICULAR BIGEMINY (i.e. PVC every other beat)—COMMON CAUSES:

"I HATE Jimmy" (bigeminy)

I schemia

H ypoxia

A lkalosis/acidosis

T hyrotoxicosis

E lectrolyte imbalance

VFIB/PULSELESS VT: MEDICATIONS: **AMPLE Voltage!**

A miodarone

M agnesium

P rocainamide

L idocaine

E pinephrine

V asopressin

VIPoma: **DASH** to **WC**[*]**!**

D   elta cells hyperproduce VIP (vasoactive intestinal peptide); these are the same cells responsible for somatostatinoma

A   chlorhydria

S   omatostatin drug of choice for control of diarrhea

H   yperglycemia in half the patients (secondary to hypokalemia- and VIP-induced glycogenolysis in the liver)

to

W   atery diarrhea, profuse secretory with frequent dehydration, hypotension, flushing, and ↓K+

C   alcemia ↑ in 2/3 ^{rds} of patients;
C̲olicky abdominal pain in nature (so-called "pancreatic cholera")

[*]   "WC", as in the European "wash closet" for toilet/bathroom!

VITAMIN K- DEPENDENT COAGULATION FACTORS:

"Sticky Coags: 1972"

S   protein deficiency or defect

C   protein deficiency or defect

1   Factor 10

9   Factor 9

7   Factor 7

2   Factor 2

ANTIBIOTIC / ANTIFUNGAL INTERACTIONS WITH WARFARIN: STIFF CRAMP

S   ulfonamides

T   etracyclines

I   soniazid

F   luoroquinolones

F   ulvicin (griseofulvin)

C ephalosporins
R ifampin
A zole antifungals
M acrolides
P enicillens

WEGENER'S GRANULOMATOSIS: W.E.G.E.N.E.R.S.

V Vasculitis, (c-ANCA +); re: "Yes, <u>We c-AN</u> !"
E ye complications: conjunctivitis and episcleritis; ptosis;
G ranulomas, necrotizing
E ar complications: serous otitis, sensory-neural deafness, mastoiditis
N eurologic complications: multiple mononeuropathy, cranial nerve palsies, peripheral neuropathies, cerebral infarcts, system (33%) seizures, transverse myelitis;
<u>N</u>asal complications: <u>bloody nasal discharge</u>; rhinorrhea
E osinophils (CBC & biopsy), if seen, point to another, often difficult-to-distinguish vasculitis & pulmonary-renal syndrome: Churg-Strauss (also usually p-ANCA)
R enal complications: Focal segmental Glomerulonephritis
<u>R</u>heumatologic complications: arthralgia, symmetric polyarthritis of small and large joints; <u>R</u>espiratory: infiltrates and/or nodules, which are often *bilateral and cavitary*; cough, hemoptysis, SOB
S addle-nose deformity; <u>S</u>inusitis (paranasal); <u>S</u>kin lesions: . These often have the appearance of small red or purple raised areas or blister-like lesions, ulcers, or nodules that may or may not be painful; <u>S</u>teroids (+ cyclophosphamide) & <u>S</u>MX-TMP in treatment

WERNICKE-KORSAKOFF SYNDROME: CAT CROAKS

C* onfusion
A* taxia
T* hiamine treatment

C onfabulation
R etrograde amnesia
O* ptho: Ophthalmoplegia; nystagmus
A nterograde amnesia
K orsakoff's psychosis
S yndrome in alcoholics

* Wernicke's is acute phase (CAT + O); Korsakoff's is chronic phase.

WHIPPLE'S DISEASE: "WHIP F'N SADAM !"   **or**   "WHIP ALAN Silly !"

W eight loss

H yperpigmentation of skin

I nfection by Tropheryma Whippelii, a gram + bacillus

P AS positive granules within macrophages

F ever

N eurologic complications

S erositis

A bdominal pain

D iarrhea

A denopathy; <u>A</u>ntibiotics (initial IV Ceftriaxone 2g bid + Streptomycin 1g qd *then*: PO x 1 year with either Bactrim ds bid or Cefixime 400 qd)

M igratory arthralgias

or

W eight loss

H yperpigmentation of skin

I nfection by Tropheryma Whippelii , a gram + bacillus; Increased temp.

P AS positive granules within macrophages

A bdominal pain; <u>A</u>ntibiotics (initial IV Ceftriaxone 2g bid + Streptomycin 1g qd *then*: PO x 1 year with either Bactrim ds bid or Cefixime 400 qd)

L ymphadenopathy

A rthralgias, migratory

N eurologic complications

S teatorrhea

WILSON'S DISEASE: "C of madness"

C opper excretion ↓ in the biliary system and is subsequently deposited in a variety of tissues

C hronic hepatitis

C opper in the serum (free copper), urine, and liver are all increased

C eruloplasmin (carrier protein for Cu) is decreased in 95% of cases

C orneal rings (Kaiser-Fleischer; a brownish pigmented ring at the edge of the cornea)

C omplications, neuropsychiatric → eg flapping tremor; chorea; rigidity; dysarthria; parkinsonism; abnormal gait; inappropriate and uncontrollable grinning {risus sardonicus: ('sea of madness')}, and drooling.

C oombs' negative hemolytic anemia

C helation with lifelong oral penicillamine increases urinary Cu excretion

ZOLLINGER-ELLISON SYNDROME: G.A.S.T.R.I.N.O.M.A.S. *

G astrinoma (ectopic <u>G</u>-cell tumor with hypersecretion of gastrin). 2/3rds of gastrinomas are malignant. They is usually found in the pancreatic head (60%) or duodenum (30%); <u>G</u>astric folds prominent.

A bdominal Pain.

S teatorrhea results from inactivation of pancreatic lipase and precipitation of bile salts and is a common presentation.

T reatment: H2-receptor blockers / proton pump inhibitors + somatostatin, and surgery; Interferon-alfa has been reported to result in biochemical responses, and to induce tumor stabilization in 20 to 40 percent of patients with gastrointestinal neuroendocrine tumors, including gastrinoma. Gastrinomas are surgically resectable in 20-25%. Prognosis: If the resection is curative→ the patient can expect a normal life expectancy; if not→ the average life expectancy is only 2 years.

R ecurrent or Recalcitrant (poorly responsive to the usual treatment) duodenal ulcers as well as post-bulbar or multiple ulcers should make you suspect gastrinoma; a single duodenal ulceration, however, is the most common radiographic finding in ZES. As for the 90% of ZES patients with PUD, most (75 percent) are in the first portion of the duodenum, 14 percent in the distal duodenum, and 11 percent in the jejunum

I ncreased serum fasting gastrin level. In the presence of gastric acid (ie, a gastric pH below 5.0), a serum gastrin value greater than 1000 pg/mL is virtually diagnostic of the disorder.) is the most sensitive and specific test (although hypergastrinemia is noted in several other disorders, including: pernicious anemia and chronic atrophic gastritis)

N ephrolithiasis/hypercalcemia—when MEN I associatedGastrinoma cells often contain secretory granules filled with other Neuroendocrine peptides such as vasoactive intestinal peptide, insulin, and glucagon.

O ctreotide (somatostatin analog)—role in diagnosis and treatment. As a diagnostic tool, remember, since most gastrinomas contain somatostatin receptors, an octreotide scan is an important tool for identifying gastrinomas (metastatic; less useful for primary). Octreotide has been shown to be beneficial in progressive, metastatic gastrinoma;

M EN I associated in ¼- ½ of the gastrinomas (remember MEN I = pituitary hyperplasia or adenoma; pancreatic islet cell hyperplasia or adenoma or carcinoma; parathyroid hyperplasia or adenoma)

A chlorhydria (eg, in patients with pernicious Anemia or Atrophic gastritis), which can also give hypergastrinemia, must be ruled out (✓gastric pH)

S ecretin test→ normal gastrin (↓) response in patients with simple duodenal ulcer (secretin normally inhibits gastrin); Paradoxical ↑ in gastrin response with ZES.

* **Remember**, <u>too</u>, as with essentially all of the GI endocrine tumors (pancreatic islet cell tumors), this is an **APUD** tumor (recall the embryological origins of most GI endocrine tumors):_ **_that's_** → **Abdominal Pain, Ulcers, Diarrhea**. 50% of cases present with diarrhea or steatorrhea. _Diarrhea_ results from large amounts of HCL secreted and may precede the ulcer symptoms. _Steatorrhea_ results from inactivation of pancreatic lipase and precipitation of bile salts.

THE IMPORTANT ZOONOSES: G! SCARY PETS !

G iardia

S pirochetes (Borrelia burgdorferi; Leptospirosis)

C ryptosporidiosis; Campylobacter; Capnocytophaga, Coxiella burnetti (Q fever); Chlamydia psittaci

A nthrax (Bacillus anthracis); Afipia felis (cat scratch disease—also Bartonella henselae)

R abies; Rickettsiae (see section on Rickettsiae)

Y ersinia entercolitica (and Y. pestis for that matter)

P sittacosis; Pasteurella multocida; Peliosis hepatis (Bartonella henselae again)

E Coli 0157H7; Erysipeloid (Erysipelothrix rhusiopathiae)

T oxoplasmosis; Tularemia (Francisella tularensis); Tick-borne diseases

S cabies; Salmonella (nontyphoidal); Sporothrix schenkii

T.U.R.D.O.

APPENDIX

A Convenient Summary Of The Over 400 Preceding Mnemonics

☞ **ALPHABETIZED** BY CLINICAL ENTITY

☞ QUICK **PAGE LOCATOR** !

☞ USE IT TO HELP YOU **QUICKLY LOCATE:**

    1. *Your favorite mnemonics and ...*

    2. *The information you want <u>now</u> !*

APPENDIX: SUMMARY OF MNEMONICS HEREIN
ALPHABETIZED BY CLINICAL TOPIC

CLINICAL TOPIC	MNEMONIC	PAGE
A-a (ALVEOLAR-ARTERIAL) GRADIENT: DIFFERENTIAL	VSD	1
ALLERGIC BRONCHOPULMONARY ASPERGILLOSIS (ABPA)	ABPA PIES	1
ABDOMINAL ANGINA (INTESTINAL ANGINA)	CLAMPS	2
ACE INHIBITOR—CONTRAINDICATIONS:	ACE wRAP	2
ACHALASIA:	BEAST, MD	2
ACQUIRED ANTITHROMBIN III DEFICIENCY: CAUSES	NO PHD	3
ACQUIRED DISORDERS ASSOCIATED WITH HYPERHOMOCYSTINEMIA:	"HYPER C.H.A.D."	3
ACROMEGALY—_Clinical Presentation_	PM SNACK	4
ACTIVATED CHARCOAL—CONTRAINDICATIONS:	CHARCOAL FLAME!	4
ACUTE MESENTERIC ISCHEMIA:	A GHOST	5
ALLOPURINOL TOXICITIES:	FREE	5
ALLOPURINOL—INDICATIONS:	SORE MTP	5
ADRENOCORTICAL FAILURE	(Turbo Notes)	6
ALPHA-1 ANTITRYPSIN DEFICIENCY:	ABE'S CHEST	7
ALZHEIMER'S DISEASE: WARNING SIGNS FOR EARLY / OPTIMAL RECOGNITION	OPTIMAL	8
ALZHEIMER'S: 4 DRUGS COMMONLY USED IN RX	CARE	8
AMEBIC LIVER ABSCESS	"Ame is looking for a normal, single, male, Mr. Right"!	8
AMIODARONE: POTENTIAL TOXICITIES	PHOTO	9
AML, TYPE 3 (M3)—KEY FEATURES	D.A.T.A.	9
AMYLOIDOSIS: AA vs. AL: WHICH IS WHICH?	AA	10
AMYLOIDOSIS: β2-MICROGLOBULIN VARIANT	C.L.A.P.	10
ANCA: WEGENER'S GRANULOMATOSIS	c-ANCA (Remember, "Yes, WE c-AN")	10

APPENDIX OF MNEMONICS

CLINICAL TOPIC	MNEMONIC	PAGE
ANCA: GOODPASTURE'S disease	p-ANCA	10
ANCA: POLYARTERITIS NODOSA (PAN)	p-AN	10
ANEMIA OF CHRONIC DISEASE	3C's	11
ANEMIAS: MACROCYTIC	BIG BERTHA'S or B. FRESH !	11
ANEMIAS: HYPOCHROMIC, MICROCYTIC	"A L.I.T. Mic"	12
ANEMIAS: NORMOCYTIC, NORMOCHROMIC	Losing it, Lysing, Low production	12
ANION GAP ACIDOSIS: CAUSES	KUSSMAUL; CMUD PILES	12
ANKYLOSING SPONDYLITIS: SUMMARY OF KEY FEATURES	A.S. M.E.M.O.R.I.E.S.	13
ANKYLOSING SPONDYLITIS: RADIOGRAPHIC FINDINGS	"Cover all your B.A.S.E.S."	13
ANTIARRHYTHMICS, CLASS III VAUGHN-WILLIAMS MEMBERS:	BASIC	14
ANTICHOLINERGIC SYNDROME	"Dry as a bone; red as a beet; blind as a bat; mad as a hatter; hot as hades"	14
CHOLINERGIC SYNDROME	S-L-U-D-G-E	14
ANTIPHOSPHOLIPID ANTIBODY SYNDROME: CLINICAL FEATURES:	VITAL	15
AORTIC STENOSIS: SX AS PROGNOSTICATORS	A.S. FAILURE	15
APLASTIC ANEMIA: KEY FEATURES	"I.D.I.O.T.S. pay with plastic!"	15
ARGYLL-ROBERTSON PUPILS	Aka the "PROSTITUTE'S PUPIL" because it "accommodates but does not react."	16
ARTHRITIDES/ARTHRITIS—MAJOR CAUSES	CHRISTO!	16
AFIB: CAUSES	PIRATE SHIP	16
AUSTIN-FLINT & GRAHAM-STEEL MURMURS:	AI & MS	17
AUTOIMMUNE HEPATITIS:	GAY LASS	17
AVASCULAR (ASEPTIC) NECROSIS:	GERIATRIC HIPS	18
SITE OF ACTION FROM PRE- TO POST-SYNAPTIC:	(B→O→M)	18
BABESIOSIS:	ASHEN TICK !	19
BACK PAIN—CAUSES:	SADISM	20
BEHCET'S SYNDROME:	BEHCET'S	20
BEHCET'S DISEASE-- CLINICAL SPECTRUM:	CUT OPENS	21
BEHCET'S SYNDROME—DIAGNOSTIC SIGNS:	CUTE SPECS	21
BLEEDING TIME– KEY CAUSES:	ADD 'M UP	22
BLOODY DIARRHEA or FECAL LEUKOCYTES: BACTERIAL CAUSES	"YE^{3}S^2, Can Cause!"	22
BOERHAAVE'S SYNDROME:	DAMN PERFS!	22

CLINICAL TOPIC	MNEMONIC	PAGE
BOTULISM COMPLICATIONS:	6 D's	23
BRONCHIECTASIS—CAUSES:	ASCERTAIN RISK	23
BRUCELLOSIS:	HALF-ASSED	24
BUERGER'S DISEASE:	SURG TIPS	24
CAPLAN SYNDROME—KEY FEATURES:	CAPLAN	25
CARCINOMAS THAT METASTASIZE TO BONE:	"These Kinds Metastasize T.O. Bone—Poor Lad !"	25
CARDIAC SYNDROME X: MAIN CLINICAL FEATURES:	MANAGE	25
CARDIAC TAMPONADE: CLINICAL MANIFESTATIONS	TAPPED HER	26
CARDIOGENIC SHOCK FOLLOWING ACUTE MI: IMPORTANT CAUSES	PAL FITS	26
CELIAC SPRUE (GLUTEN SENSITIVE ENTEROPATHY):	I HOARD GAS	27
CELIAC SPRUE: GRAINS TO AVOID	*These should raise your* BROW	27
CEREBRAL ANEURYSMS-- WHICH MEDICAL CONDITIONS PREDISPOSE ?	SEARCH ME !	28
CEREBRAL INFARCTION: HEMATOLOGIC DISEASES ASSOCIATED	SLEPT W/ M.e	28
CHARCOT'S JOINTS—COMMON DISORDERS PREDISPOSING:	STOMPED!	29
CHLAMYDIA PSITTACOSIS:	AH! FACTS!	29
CHLORIDE-RESISTANT (or Chloride-Unresponsive) METABOLIC ALKALOSES:	"CHLORIDE"	30
CHRONIC ATROPHIC GASTRITIS ('Nonerosive Gastritis'): TYPES A & B	(Turbo Notes)	30
CHRONIC HEPATITIS—IMPORTANT CAUSES:	ABCDEF	31
CRF: SUPPLEMENTS TO CONSIDER	BCDE	31
CHURG-STRAUSS SYNDROME:	CHEAP PORN	31
CHURG-STRAUSS SYNDROME: ACR CRITERIA:	NAB PEN	32
CIRRHOSIS—KEY CAUSES:	WHAT BS !	33
CLUBBING #1:	CLUBBING	33
CLUBBING #2—CAUSES:	C5 NAILS (as in "See 5 nails")	33
COMA—ETIOLOGIES:	VICTIM	34
HTN + COMORBID CONDITION ☞ CHOOSE AN ACE INHIBITOR:	SHARED	34
HTN + COMORBID CONDITION ☞ BETA-BLOCKERS MAKE AN …	IMPACT	34
HTN + COMORBID CONDITION ☞ CHOOSE A DIURETIC:	CIAO !	34
COMPLICATIONS OF ACUTE *OR* CHRONIC PANCREATITIS:	"P" for Pancreas	35
CONGENITAL ADRENAL HYPERPLASIA: 17 α hydroxylase deficiency	Hyper teenager (17)	36

APPENDIX OF MNEMONICS

CLINICAL TOPIC	MNEMONIC	PAGE
CONGENITAL ADRENAL HYPERPLASIA: 21-hydroxylase deficiency	Becoming a man (virilization) at age 21	36
COMMON EXAMPLES OF CONTACT DERMATITIS:	RE: PLANT	37
COOMB'S POSITIVE AUTOIMMUNE HEMOLYSIS:	"Mmmm, **cold** beer. My **Compliments** to your bar." (beer→intrahepatic)	37
COMMON CAUSES OF COPD:	ABCDE	38
CREST SYNDROME:	CREST	38
CRYOGLOBULINEMIA: TYPE I: CLINICAL ASSOCIATIONS:	I.M.	38
CRYOGLOBULINEMIA Type I / CRYOGLOBULINS	M's	39
CRYOGLOBULINEMIA*—Types II & III:	P's	40
CUSHING'S SYNDROME:	Steroid M.A.S.O.C.H.I.S.T. !	41
CUSHING'S DIFFERENTIALS & DIAGNOSTICS	(Turbo Notes)	41-42
DERMATOLOGY QUICK- LINKS ™	SKIN DISEASE AS A MANIFESTATION OF MALIGNANCY...	43
DERMATOLOGY QUICK- LINKS ™	CUTANEOUS MANIFESTATIONS IN INFECTIOUS DISEASE	44
DERMATOLOGY QUICK- LINKS ™	SELECTIVE CUTANEOUS DISEASES IN AIDS	45
DERMATOLOGY QUICK- LINKS ™	CUTANEOUS SIGNS OF SYSTEMIC DISEASE	46
CYSTIC FIBROSIS:	PINK SCHNAPPS	48
DERMATOMYOSITIS:	SH!T HAPPENS	49
DERMATOMYOSITIS: CARRY AN ↑ RISK OF THESE TUMORS:	GO CLUB!	49
DIALYSIS INDICATIONS	I HAVE 2 PEE	50
DIC: IMPORTANT CLINICAL ASSOCIATIONS	S.L.O.T.S.	50
DIGOXIN LEVEL: INDICATIONS FOR CHECKING	A.T. R.I.S.K.	50
DIPTHERIA:	D.I.P.T.H.E.R.I.A.	51
DLCO ↓: DIFFERENTIAL DIAGNOSIS:	RE: PISA ↓	52
DLCO ↑: DIFFERENTIAL DIAGNOSIS	"S.O.A.P. up ! " **or** S.H.A.P.E. up!	52
DMARD THERAPY IN RHEUMATIC DISEASE:	GOLD PILE SCAM:	53
DRUG-INDUCED PERIPHERAL NEUROPATHIES:	DITCH MAP	54
DRUGS CAUSING: PULMONARY INFILTRATES	BN Gold CHAMP!	54
DRUGS FREQUENTLY ASSOCIATED WITH ESOPHAGITIS	QUINcy PAID 'N Cash	54
DRUGS THAT CAN ↑: CYCLOSPORINE (CSA) LEVELS)	Stacking the DECK	55
DUKE'S CLASSIFICATION FOR COLORECTAL CA:	Don't B2 SERious!	55
DYSPHAGIA FOR SOLID OR LIQUID FOODS:	SAD	55
DYSPHAGIA FOR SOLID FOODS ONLY:	CRaP	55

CLINICAL TOPIC	MNEMONIC	PAGE
ECTHYMA GANGRENOSUM:	PAINLESS	56
EKG: AN *EASIER* WAY TO FIGURE AXIS!	"RULE OF THUMBS"…	57
ERYTHEMA NODOSUM: ASSOCIATED CONDITIONS:	Yer Leg BUMPS	56
ENCAPSULATED ORGANISMS:	CAN SPIKE T !	57
EP STUDY: INDICATIONS	SCAR	57
EOSINOPHILIA—DIFFERENTIAL:	PANIC	58
ERYTHEMAS: ALL TOGETHER NOW!	"E Gads!!"	58
ESOPHAGEAL SQUAMOUS CELL CA—RISK FACTORS #1:	E.A.T. T.I.P.S.	58
ESOPHAGEAL SQUAMOUS CELL CA—RISK FACTORS #2:	A.S. S.P.E.L.T !	59
EXTRAARTICULAR MANIFESTATIONS OF RA:	MD Felt SPLEAN	59
EXTRAVASCULAR HEMOLYSIS:	"H.E.M.A.T.ology *Extras*!"	59
INTRAVASCULAR HEMOLYSIS:	MAPS	60
FACTOR XIII DEFICIENCY: KEY FEATURES	FOUND Postop !	60
FACTORS INVOLVED IN THE: FINAL COMMON PATHWAY:	"2 X 5 = 10"	60
FAMILIAL HYPOCALCIURIC HYPERCALCEMIA (FHH):	AMOR'S PUB	61
FARMER'S LUNG:	BET THE FARM	61
FELTY'S SYNDROME	Felt L.U.M.P.S.	62
FEVER + PURPURA: DIFFERENTIAL	MERSA	62
FIBROMYALGIA: KEY THERAPEUTIC OPTIONS:	PABST !	62
FIBROMYALGIA: SUMMARY OF KEY POINTS:	F.A.C.H.E.I.N.G.	63
GASTRIC CANCER: CONDITIONS THAT PREDISPOSE	SAM's PUB!	63
GIARDIASIS: IMPORTANT FEATURES:	WARM FLOW	64
GLOMERULAR DISEASE WITH ↓ COMPLEMENT:	Cold ALPINE	64
GLUCAGONOMA:	SCAN WARDS	65
GOUT: CONDITIONS ASSOCIATED:	"That's a *HARD* 1 !"	65
GOUT: COMMON CAUSES OF URIC ACID UNDEREXCRETION:	"That's *HARD* 2 !"	65
GOUT: COMMON CAUSES OF OVERPRODUCTION:	*MORE HELP*	66
GRAM POSITIVE RODS:	LANCES	66
GRAPEFRUIT JUICE: INTERACTING DRUGS:	C. A. MISHAP or CLASH!	66
GYNECOMASTIA: KEY CAUSES:	MAIDEN STOCK or DEMONIC TASK	67
GYNECOMASTIA: DRUGS THAT CAN PREDISPOSE	CDC's IM DEPT	68
HAART: COMBINATIONS TO AVOID:	4Z extra point	68
HAART: COMBINATIONS TO AVOID:	C.I.	
HAART: COMBINATIONS TO AVOID:	INSAne	
HAART: COMBINATIONS TO AVOID:	3,4 out the door	
HAPTOGLOBIN, HEMOSIDERIN, HEMOGLOBINURIA, HEMOSIDERINURIA:	(Turbo Notes)	69
HEMOCHROMATOSIS—IMPORTANT COMPLICATIONS:	I. A.C.H.E. !	69

APPENDIX OF MNEMONICS

CLINICAL TOPIC	MNEMONIC	PAGE
HEMOCHROMATOSIS—*IRREVERSIBLE* COMPLICATIONS:	H.A.G.	69
HEMOLYSIS DUE TO CELLULAR DEFECTS:	SHIP	69
HEMOLYTIC ANEMIA: KEY LABS	CRUSH Labs	70
HEMOLYTIC CONDITIONS: CONGENITAL	H.E.M.e	70
HEMOLYTIC CONDITIONS: ACQUIRED:	"Acquired a M.A.P."	71
HEMOLYTIC ANEMIAS: GENERAL:	SHEER IT	71
HEMOPTYSIS—MOST COMMON CAUSES:	B.L.T.	71
HENOCH-SHÖNLEIN PURPURA	PAINS or GAP USA	72
HEPATIC VEIN THROMBOSIS MAY COMPLICATE THESE:	HOPING	72
HEPATITIS B—KEY CLINICAL ASSOCIATIONS TO KNOW:	"B A CHAMP!"	73
HEPATITIS C—KEY CLINICAL ASSOCIATIONS TO KNOW:	"C. Mi Pita Me.L.T.S." "C. S.P.iL.T. M.ilk"	73
HEPATITIS C	THE 'RULE OF 20s'	74
HEPATOMEGALY + HEART FAILURE—NOT JUST CHF:	CHA CHA	74
HEPATORENAL SYNDROME:	FACT DUMP!	74
HEREDITARY HEMORRHAGIC TELANGIECTASIA:	F.A.T.A.L. O.N.E.	75
HEREDITARY ANGIONEUROTIC EDEMA (HANE):	F.A.T. L.I.P.S.	76
HIV: IMPORTANT, COMMON DERMATOLOGIC INFECTIONS	C. Z.O.M.B.I.E.S.	77
HIV: INFECTIOUS CAUSES OF GI DISEASE	CHIC MAG	78
HLA-DR- ASSOCIATED CONDITIONS:	DR. MALIGNANT	79
HYPERTROPHIC PULMONARY OSTEOARTHROPATHY: KEY FEATURES OF HPOA	PRICE/LB	79
HYPERCALCEMIA—CAUSES:	MD SET HIP	80
HYPERKALEMIA: KNOW THESE IMPORTANT CAUSES:	RHABDO	80
HYPOMAGNESEMIA: KEY CAUSES:	ABCDEFGH	80
HYPERPROLACTINEMIA: CAUSES	DAPHNE'S PEACHES	81
HYPERPARATHYROIDISM; HYPOPARATHYROIDISM	(Turbo Notes)	82
HYPERTROPHIC CARDIOMYOPATHY (HCM): CHARACTERISTIC ECHOCARDIOGRAPHIC FINDINGS	SAM ASH	82
INDICATIONS FOR IABP (Intra-Aortic Balloon Pump):	IABP'S	82
IDIOPATHIC INTRACRANIAL HTN (IIH):	PSEUDO HINTS	83
IDIOPATHIC INTRACRANIAL HTN (IIH): Endocrinologic risk factors	ACHE FROM	83
IDIOPATHIC INTRACRANIAL HTN (IIH): KEY DRUGS ASSOCIATED	TOAST	83
IMPORTANT CAUSES OF ↑ ACE LEVELS:	A.C.E. T.R.A.M.P.S.	84
INDICATIONS FOR SURGERY IN INFECTIVE ENDOCARDITIS:	SHAVE PAP !	84
IBD: LIVER DYSFUNCTION IN	CCCHHH	84
IBD: EXTRAINTESTINAL FEATURES	E. PEARLS !	85
IBD AND ARTHRITIS	(Turbo Notes)	85
INTERVENTIONS THAT HAVE BEEN SHOWN TO ↓ MORTALITY AFTER MI:	"Take A STAB at it"	86

CLINICAL TOPIC	MNEMONIC	PAGE
INVASIVE BACTERIAL DIARRHEAS	"Yer V.I.C.E.S.!"	86
IRREGULARLY IRREGULAR PULSE: DIFFERENTIAL DIAGNOSIS	S.P.A.M.	87
IRRITABLE BOWEL SYNDROME—KEY FEATURES:	IBS DIAPER	87
ISCHEMIC COLITIS:	WASTING	88
KARTAGENER'S SYNDROME	(Immotile Cilia Syndrome):	88
KAWASAKI DISEASE:	CECIL'S FAV	89
KAWASAKI'S DISEASE: CLINICAL MANIFESTATIONS:	C FEVERS	89
KLINEFELTER'S SYNDROME:	BIG SHAME	90
LEFT/RIGHT ATRIAL ENLARGEMENT	"LEFT → LENGTH; RIGHT → HEIGHT"	90
LETHARGY/MALAISE—CAUSES:	LUNAR TIDE	90
LEGIONNAIRES' DISEASE:	"Lung, Liver, Lytes, Loose BMs"	91
LEUKEMOID REACTIONS: DISTINGUISHING FEATURES FROM CML:	Not CML !	91
LITHIUM--SIDE EFFECTS:	LITHIUM	91
LOW-VOLTAGE EKG: CAUSES	ECG LOST	92
LOWER LOBE INFILTRATES—IMPORTANT CAUSES:	B HAPPI	92
LUPUS ANTICOAGULANT: COMMON DIFFERENTIAL:	Drug-using L.I.A.R.	92
LUNG CARCINOMA: SENTRAL BROCHOGENIC CARCINOMAS	SMALL, Squamous cell	93
LUNG CA & HYPERTROPHIC OSTEOARTHOPATHY	Peripheral → Peripheral	93
LUNG CARCINOMA: SMALL CELL	"CASES"	93
LUNG CARCINOMA & GYNECOMASTIA	LARGE CELL	93
LUNG CARCINOMA—NOTORIOUS COMPLICATIONS:	"Gee S.H.A.P.E.S."	93
LUNG CA STAGING Stage IIIB →Chemo + XRT	"B" →"Bilateral " & Contralateral → Chemo)	94
LYMPHOPROLIFERATIVE DISORDERS: 4 IMPORTANT ONES:	C$_a$LL 4 H$_e$LP	95
MALIGNANCIES ASSOCIATED WITH AIDS:	C.H.A.L.K.	95
MECKEL'S DIVERTICULUM:	RULE OF 2'S	95
MEN I Syndrome—aka Wermer Syndrome	1 MAN (MEN I) in a panic (panc) in a parachute (parathyroid) over Pittsburgh (pituitary tumor)	96
MEN IIA Syndrome[2]—aka Sipple Syndrome	a "Pair of (Parathyroid; also implies MEN II) medium (medullary) feet (pheo)"	96
METABOLIC ALKALOSIS ☞ check the URINE CHLORIDE	(Turbo Notes)	96
METABOLIC BONE DISEASES: IMPORTANT LABORATORY COMPARISON ON THE BOARDS	(Turbo Table)	97
MOCLONAL GAMMOPATHY OF UNDETERMINED SIGNIFICANCE (MGUS):	CALM	97
MITRAL STENOSIS: KEY PHYSICAL FINDINGS	"Pretty Loud DEMO"	98

APPENDIX OF MNEMONICS

CLINICAL TOPIC	MNEMONIC	PAGE
MITRAL STENOSIS: SACRED PRINCIPLES OF MANAGEMENT	SACRED	98
MRI FOR THE BOARDS: IMPORTANT INDICATIONS	"That's 'S' as in 'S.C.A.N.'"	99
MULTIPLE MYELOMA—KEY FEATURES #1:	CARPE DIEM !	99
MULTIPLE MYELOMA—KEY FEATURES (#2):	CALCIUM	100
MYELOMA KIDNEY: MECHANISMS OF RENAL INSUFFICIENCY:	U CLAP	101
MUSCULOSKELETAL DISORDERS ASSOCIATED WITH MALIGNANCY:	VOTED ALL CORPS	101
MITRAL VALVE PROLAPSE: CLINICAL CORRELATES	RAW HEMP	101
MYASTHENIA GRAVIS:	"WE ARE TIRED!"	102
MYCOPLASMA PNEUMONIAE:	M.P. MENACE	103
MYELOFIBROSIS:	SPLEEN TIP	103
MYOCARDIAL INFARCTIONS—INTERVENTIONS SHOWN TO ↓ MORTALITY:	PABST	104
"NAIL YOUR LINES": Here's how:	MUehrcke's LINES; Mee's LINES; Beau's LINES	104
NON-ANION GAP ACIDOSIS:	CRAP	104
NEPHROLOGY PEARLS	(Turbo Notes)	105-106
NEPHROTIC DISORDERS: BASIC FINDINGS:	LEAP Over	106
NEPHROTIC SYNDROME—CAUSES:	OH DAVID !	107
NEPHRITIC DISORDERS:	PAIRS	107
NEPHRITIC AND NEPHROTIC SYNDROMES: COMPLEMENT LEVELS IN	You lie 'down in PM' 'BAR none' 'SLIM down' GHOST (paranormal)	107
NEPHROLOGY: WHICH CASTS MEAN WHAT ?!	(Turbo Table)	108
NEUROLEPTICS	NEUROLEPTICS	109
NEUROLEPTICS: 4 MAIN clinical features:	HARM	109
NON-HODGKINS LYMPHOMA: POOR PROGNOSTICATORS	ALE on TAP	108
NORMAL PRESSURE HYDROCEPHALUS:	AID	109
OBSTRUCTIVE SLEEP APNEA—CLINICAL FEATURES:	PA SNORES !	110
OCTREOTIDE INDICATIONS: Label & Off-Label Uses:	D.I.A.B.E.T.E.S.*	110
ORAL & GENITAL ULCERATION--DIFFERENTIAL:	B.E.H.C.E.T.'S.	111
OCULOMUCOCUTANEOUS SYNDROMES: IMPORTANT ONES:	SUPERB !	111
ORAL LEUKOPLAKIA:	PERSISTS	111
OSGOOD-SCHLATTERS DISEASE:	EXCRUTIATING	112
OSMOLAR GAP	(Turbo Notes)	113
OSTEOARTHRITIS—RADIOGRAPHIC SIGNS:	Bone LOSS	113
OSTEOMALACIA—Important Causes:	I.D. AFGHAN CAMPS	113
OSTEOMALACIA: Key Features:	PALM PDA	114

CLINICAL TOPIC	MNEMONIC	PAGE
OSTEOPOROSIS—RISK FACTORS:	M/F CLASH	114
P. VERA—KEY FEATURES:	PHLEBOTOMY	115
PAGET'S DISEASE OF THE BONE:	C. PAINS!	116
PAGET'S DISEASE:	PAGET'S CONT'D	116
PALPABLE PURPURA: DIFFERENTIAL DIAGNOSIS	CRIBSHEET	117
PANCREATITIS, ACUTE: CLINICAL FEATURES	AMYLASE	117
PANCREATITIS: RANSON'S CRITERIA: *AT TIME OF ADMISSION OR DIAGNOSIS:*	"Andre Will Golf Laguna Soon"	118
PANCREATITIS: RANSON'S CRITERIA: *DURING INITIAL 48 HOURS:*	*Ranson's* BASeline BUNdl Sure CAn Help Out"	118
PANCREATITIS, CHRONIC: CLINICAL FEATURES:	C MAIDS (think 'C' for chronic as in "old maids!")	118
PANCREATITIS: CULPRIT DRUGS	"PD FAST VET" (as in "Pretty Fast corVETte"):	119
PARACENTESIS: EXUDATIVE ASCITES	EX (also, *everything* EXceeds*)	119
PARACENTESIS: TRANSUDATIVE EFFUSIONS:	MUNCHES	119
PARACENTESIS: IMPORTANT LABS TO REMEMBER:	5C's:	120
PARVOVIRUS B19:	SLAP CHEEK	120
PATHOLOGICAL 'Q' WAVES: IMPORTANT CAUSES	KIMCHI PIE	121
PEA (Pulseless Electrical Activity): REVERSIBLE CAUSES W/ ACUTE INTERVENTIONS:	5-HT$_4$	121
PELIOSIS HEPATIS*—CLINICAL ASSOCIATIONS:	CAPO	121
PEMPHIGUS VULGARIS:	ALOT OF PAINS	122
PERIPHERAL NEUROPATHIES—DIFFERENTIAL:	DIABETES	122
PERNICIOUS ANEMIA—LABS:	"MAMA HAS pernicious anemia.	123
PEUTZ-JEGHERS DISEASE:	"P&J or H.A.M.?"	123
PHEOCHROMOCYTOMA	*RULE OF 10's:*	124
PITYRIASIS ROSEA:	HERPES	124
PITYRIASIS VERSICOLOR (TINEA VERSICOLOR):	SPOT FACTS	124
QUICK DIFFS ™: QUICK DIFFERENTIALS FOR PLEURAL FLUID ANALYSIS :	(Turbo Section)	126
PLEURAL FLUID ANALYSIS : LOW GLUCOSE or pH	TRAMPLE down	126
PLEURAL FLUID ANALYSIS : AMYLASE ↑:	"Amy's PERM"	126
PLEURAL FLUID ANALYSIS : BLOODY PLEURAL FLUID:	"Bloody TAMPon"	126
PLEURAL EFFUSIONS: COMMON MALIGNANT EFFUSIONS TO KNOW	Meta S.L.O.B. **or** MO' LBS !	127
PLEURAL FLUID ANALYSIS : LYMPHS PREDOMINATE (Nymphs predominate?):	LiVe FAST!	127
PLEURAL FLUID ANALYSIS : EOSINOPHILS ↑ IN PLEURAL FLUID:	ABCD	127

APPENDIX OF MNEMONICS

CLINICAL TOPIC	MNEMONIC	PAGE
PLUMMER-VINSON SYNDROME:	DAMSEL	127
PML (Progressive Multifocal Leukoencephalopathy):	WHITE OUT !	128
PORTANT INDICATIONS FOR PNEUMOCOCCAL VACCINE:	HE CRAMS	128
POLYARTERITIS NODOSA (PAN):	p-ANCA	128
POLYCYSTIC KIDNEY DISEASE:	HARLEM or PALM BEACH ? (You choose!)	129
POLYCYSTIC OVARIAN SYNDROME:	OVARIAN	129
POST-GASTRECTOMY COMPLICATIONS: #1	"WE B DUMPING FAT !"	130
POST-GASTRECTOMY COMPLICATIONS: #2	6 D's	130
POST-SPLENECTOMY INFECTIONS TO KNOW	"Ca.S.H. 'M. Babe !"	131
PRIMARY BILIARY CIRRHOSIS:	PAM'S SICK	131
PARATHYROIDISM (1° HYPER...)	↑ PTH HARMS	131
PRIMARY PULMONARY HTN	CHEAPEST DRAFTS (or CARPETED SHAFTS if you like)	132
PRIMARY PULMONARY HTN : MANAGEMENT:	T.A. CODED	133
PRIMARY SCLEROSING CHOLANGITIS:	PSC CLUES	133
PROGRESSIVE SUPRANUCLEAR PALSY:	BANANA PEELS	134
↑ QT INTERVAL: MUST-KNOW CAUSES	EPITAPH	134
PSEUDOMONAS AERUGINOSA: Common Infections & Clinical Settings:	C iN HOT TUBS! (as in you "See (pseudomonas) in hottubs"	135
PSEUDOOBSTRUCTION:	MOSES	135
PULMONARY CAVITATION—COMMON CAUSES:	VIETNAM & South Korea	136
PUMONARY-RENAL SYNDROMES:	We Go 'Do' Church	136
RAYNAUD'S PHENOMENON: ASSOCIATED CONDITIONS	AMBER's VIB	136
REACTIVE ARTHRITIS—GI & GU PRECIPITANTS:	Yer. B.U.C.K.S.	137
REITER'S SYNDROME—KEY FEATURES:	C.U.A.C.K.	137
REFRACTORY CHF: DIAGNOSES TO CONSIDER	ASTHMA COPS	137
RELAPSING POLYCHONDRITIS—Summary of Key Features:	RELAPSING	138
RENAL DISEASE + JAUNDICE:	SHARP Yellow BMW	138
RENAL ENLARGEMENT: KEY CAUSES	S.C.A.N. H.A.R.D. (indeed sca well!)	138
RENAL FAILURE & HEMOPTYSIS:	"We Go PAINT the CHEST (red)"	139
RENAL TUBULAR ACIDOSES (RTAs)	(Turbo Table)	140
METABOLIC ALKALOSIS & URINE CHLORIDE	(Turbo Notes)	140

CLINICAL TOPIC	MNEMONIC	PAGE
RHEUMATIC HEART DISEASE: MAJOR AND MINOR JONES CRITERIA:	SAFER CASES	141
RHEUMATOID ARTHRITIS & PULMONARY INVOLVEMENT	SCRIP CO.	141
RHEUMATOLOGIC AUTOANTIBODIES:	(Turbo Notes)	141
RHINOCEREBRAL MUCORMYCOSIS: GENERAL	S.N.O.R.E.S. B.A.D.	142
RHINOCEREBRAL MUCORMYCOSIS: POTENTIAL COMPLICATIONS	"T.O.N.E. Deaf."	142
RICKETTSIAL DISEASES* OF MEDICAL IMPORTANCE IN NORTH AMERICA:	RQETSia	143
RISK FACTORS FOR CERVICAL CANCER:	LIPSTICK	143
ROCKY MOUNTAIN SPOTTED FEVER:	ROCKY MT. OYSTERS	144
ROSACEA	CATSUP	145
ROSACEA: COMMON AGGRAVATING FACTORS (or factors that can *TEASE* it out)	TEASE	146
SARCOIDOSIS: INDICATIONS FOR STEROIDS	P.H.O.N.I.C.S.	146
SARCOIDOSIS: KEY FEATURES	OBSCENE FACE	146
SPONTANEOUS BACTERIAL PERITONITIS (SBP):	FAT SBP	147
SCHISTOCYTES—IMPORTANT CAUSES OF MICROANGIOPATHIC HEMOLYTIC ANEMIA:	SAD PATH	147
SCLERODERMA—KEY FEATURES:	G.I. W.A.R.D.S.	147
SCROTAL MASSES:	HE VOMITS	148
SECONDARY HYPERLIPIDEMIA: IMPORTANT CAUSES	D.E.L. N.A.C.H.O.S.!	138
SECONDARY THROMBOCYTOSIS: IMPORTANT, COMMON CAUSES	"I.'M. H.O.T."	148
SEMINOMAS & NONSEMINOMAS	(Turbo Notes and Table)	149
SERONEGATIVE SPONDYLOARTHROPATHIES:	REAP	149
SEROTONIN SYNDROME—CLINICAL FEATURES:	MISMATCH	149
SEROTONIN SYNDROME: *DRUGS TO WATCH OUT FOR:*	SANDBLAST !	149
SERUM SICKNESS:	Drugs' F.A.U.L.T.	150
SERUM SICKNESS: IMPORTANT CAUSES	"B.A.D. A.S.S. Anti-Drugs"	150
SIADH: IMPORTANT CAUSES	Pituitary ADENOMA	151
SIADH-INDUCING DRUGS:	TOBASCO	151
SIADH--IMPORTANT CAUSES:	DOLPHINS	151
SICKLE CELL COMPLICATIONS:	"G.A.R.L.I.C makes me Sick A Hell" (Sickle Cell) :	152
SICKLE CELL CRISES: MAIN TYPES	M.I.S.H.A.P.	152
RHEUMATOLOGIC MANIFESTATIONS OF SICKLE CELL DISEASE:	SHAG!	153

CLINICAL TOPIC	MNEMONIC	PAGE
SOMATOSTATINOMA	**S³**	153
SOMOGYI EFFECT vs. DAWN PHENOMENON:	(Turbo Notes)	153-154
SPUR CELLS & BURR CELLS	(Turbo Notes)	154
ST DEPRESSION—CAUSES:	**MED SLIP** (when you slip, you fall *down*)	154
ST ELEVATION: CAUSES	**PHALLIC pole**	154
STATISTICS:	(Notes)	155
STEATOHEPATITIS—CAUSES:	**SPORTs ADDICT**	156
STERILE PYRURIA—CAUSES OF:	**TRACT**	156
STILL'S DISEASE:	**RASH;** Still **FAR** away	156
STREPTOCOC**K**US—IMPORTANT INFECTIONS:	**PENILE SUPPORTS**	157
STRESS ULCERS:	**Curling's vs. Cushing's:**	157
SUDDEN INCREASE IN ASCITES IN PREVIOUSLY STABLE CIRRHOSIS:	**HASHISH**	157
SUDDEN RESPIRATORY ARREST:	"Give him **SPACE!**"	158
SWEET'S SYNDROME:	"**D.A.N.A.'S. F.A.T.**" (*from eating too much Sweet's!*)	158
SYSTEMIC MASTOCYTOSIS:	**GET UP!**	159
TALL R-WAVE (R>S) IN V1 OR V2: CAUSES	"**WARN HIM DR !**"	158
TERATOGENIC DRUGS:	**FEW MORTALS**	160
THEOPHYLLINE: Conditions Which Slow the Rate of Theophylline Elimination	**COOLS** down	160
THEOPHYLLINE: DRUGS WHICH CAN INCREASE THEO LEVELS	**FACED COP**	160
THRYOID NODULES	**90% Rule Of Thumb**:	160
THIAZIDE DIURETICS: METABOLIC SIDE EFFECTS: WHICH LABS GO <u>UP</u>?	**G.L.U.**	161
THIAZIDE DIURETICS: METABOLIC SIDE EFFECTS: WHICH LABS GO <u>DOWN</u>?	**P.M.S.** (Feeling down?)	161
THROMBOCYTOPENIA: 3 BASIC PROCESSES	(Turbo Notes)	161
TICK-BORNE DISEASES (U.S.) ON THE BOARDS	**B ALERT !**	161
TICK-BORNE DISEASES → "OVERBITES", i.e. OVERLAPPING TICK BITES (WHICH TICKS ARE RESPONSIBLE FOR WHICH DISEASES)	(Turbo Table)	162
TICK-BORNE DISEASES → VENN DIAGRAM ILLUSTRATING THE SHARED RELATIONSHIPS BETWEEN TICK VECTORS & KEY DISEASES TO KNOW:	(Turbo Diagram)	163
TORSADES DE POINTES—Drugs Causing:	"**Mama Always Prays Frida 13**th**!**"	164
TOXIGENIC BACTERIAL DIARRHEAS (*watery; no fecal leukocytes*):	**CAVE B** (B for Binladen or just B for Burial !)	164

CLINICAL TOPIC	MNEMONIC	PAGE
TTP (Thrombotic Thrombocytopenic Purpura):	FAT RN	164
HUS (HEMOLYTIC UREMIC SYNDROME)	FAT RN (ie as per TTP-only drop the 'F' and the 'N')	165
TULAREMIA:	LUST 4 FACTS	165
TUMOR LYSIS SYNDROME: KEY LABS: *What goes up?*	BuLK up !	166
TUMOR LYSIS SYNDROME: KEY LABS: *What goes down?*	A.B.C.D.ecrease!	166
TURNER'S SYNDROME:	FeMaLe SHOWCASES	166
T-WAVE INVERSIONS—CAUSES OF:	DUBLIN Pub ('bottoms up?" → T wave inversions!)	167
TYPE IV RTA "vs." BARTTER'S SYNDROME:	(Turbo Notes)	167
ULCERATIVE COLITIS: RESPONSE OF COMPLICATIONS TO COLECTOMY	Positive Response vs. Stays the Same	167
UNSTABLE ANGINA: MANAGEMENT #1 (abbrev'd)	PAGAN, B.C.	168
UNSTABLE ANGINA: MANAGEMENT #2 (in greater detail):	CIGAR	168
UPPER LOBE INFILTRATES—IMPORTANT CAUSES:	TRASH	169
URICOSURIC AGENTS (eg Probenicid): INDICATIONS	4N	169
URINARY INCONTINENCE: DRUGS THAT CAN PREDISPOSE	ABCD'S	169
VALPROATE—SIDE EFFECTS:	Pee → WETLANDS	170
VENTRICULAR BIGEMINY—COMMON CAUSES:	"I HATE Jimmy" (bigeminy)	170
VFIB/PULSELESS VT: MEDICATIONS:	AMPLE Voltage!	170
VIPoma:	DASH to WC* !	171
VITAMIN K- DEPENDENT COAGULATION FACTORS:	"Sticky Coags: 1972"	171
WARFARIN: ANTIBIOTICS / ANTIFUNGALS THAT INTERACT	STIFF CRAMP	171
WEGENER'S GRANULOMATOSIS:	W.E.G.E.N.E.R.S.	172
WERNICKE-KORSAKOFF SYNDROME:	CAT CROAKS	172
WHIPPLE'S DISEASE:	"WHIP F'N SADAM !" **or** "WHIP ALAN Silly !"	173
WILSON'S DISEASE:	"C of madness"	173
ZOLLINGER-ELLISON SYNDROME #1	G.A.S.T.R.I.N.O.M.A.S.	174
ZOLLINGER-ELLISON SYNDROME #2	APUD tumor	175
ZOONOSES YOU GOTTA KNOW	G! SCARY PETS !	176

REFERENCES

1. NAIL THE BOARDS 2005-2006! 5th edition, Frontrunners Publishing/FBRI, Aliso Viejo, CA. © 2005-2006

2. FRONTRUNNERS 2005-2006 INTERNAL MEDICINE Q&A REVIEW: Companion for Board Review, 5 th edition, Frontrunners Publishing/FBRI, Aliso Viejo, CA, © 2005-2006

3. TURBO MNEMONICS FOR THE BOARDS: 2 nd edition (previous edition), Frontrunners Publishing/FBRI, Aliso Viejo, CA, © 2004

4. FRONTRUNNERS AUDIO/VISUAL SLIDE SHOWS CD-Roms.

5. UpToDate Clinical Reference Library, UpToDate, Inc., Wellesley, MA

6. The Sanford Guide to Antimicrobial Therapy, David N. Gilbert, MD, et al, 35 th ed., © 2005

7. Cecil Essentials of Medicine, 6 th edition, Andreoli, T. et al, W. B. Saunders Company, Philadelphia, PA.

8. Harrison's Principles of Internal Medicine, 16 th edition, Kasper, Braunwald, Fauci, © 2005

9. ACP Board Review Course, 1996-2005

10. Medical Knowledge Self-Assessment Program VII, VIII, IX, X, XI, and XII, XII update, American College of Physicians, Philadelphia, PA.

11. Frontrunners' Internal Medicine Board Review Course, 1996-2003, Frontrunners Board Review, Inc., New York

12. Frontrunners' WEEKEND MARATHON REVIEWS, 1996-2005, Frontrunners Board Review, Inc., New York/California

INDEX

INDEX

ℬ

INDEX

C

INDEX

INDEX

INDEX

𝒢

ℋ

INDEX

INDEX

INDEX

INDEX

INDEX

INDEX

INDEX

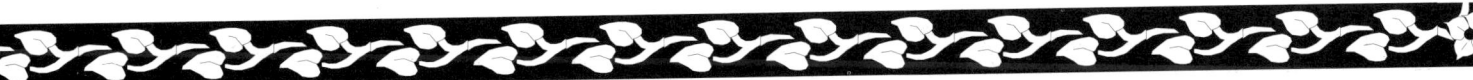

INDEX

INDEX

INDEX

T

INDEX

INDEX

Quick Order Form

YOU SHOULD KNOW WE ALSO OFFER THESE INCREDIBLE RESOURCES !! :

(Put an "X" thru the products you're interested in)

❏ **2005-2006 INTERNAL MEDICINE Q&A REVIEW FOR THE BOARDS. > 1300 Q&A TO PREPARE YOU**, © 2005-2006 ☞ $149.^{00}

❏ **2005-2006 AUDIO/VISUAL SLIDE SHOWS for the BOARDS** FEATURING ALL THE KEY IMAGES YOU'LL NEED TO KNOW IN FULL COLOR, & BEAUTIFULLY PRESENTED IN POWERPOINT, © 2005-2006
☞ $495.^{00}

❏ *Why not order a copy as a gift for a student, friend or colleague?* **TURBO MNEMONICS FOR THE BOARDS 2005-2006**: FEATURING >400 MEMORY AIDS TO THE *MOST COMMONLY ASKED* CLINICAL MATERIAL on the BOARDS. © 2005-2006 ☞ $39.^{95}

+ S&H * : $8.^{00}

TOTAL :

3 EASY ORDER OPTIONS:

1. *Fax* orders: **949-203-6178. FAX THIS FORM.**

2. *E-mail* (or info): **FRONTRUNNERS@hotmail.com**

3. *Telephone*.: **Call Toll-Free: 866-MDBOARDs or 866-IMREVIEW** V/MC/AMEX/Discover/Diners accepted.

SHIPPING ADDRESS:
(Sales tax of 7.75% will be added for all orders shipped within California)
(* Add $8.00 S&H on all orders)

Name: _____

Address: _____

City State Zip: _____

Tel/Fax/Email: _____ (emerg only)

(We can ALSO FAX your receipt /confirmation to you within 24h if you request)

PAYMENT OPTIONS: ❏ Money Order ❏ Circle CC: V/MC/AMEX/Discover/Diners

Card number: _____

Name on card: _____ Exp. Date _____

Quick Order Form

YOU SHOULD KNOW WE **ALSO** OFFER THESE **INCREDIBLE RESOURCES !!** :

(Put an "X" thru the products you're interested in)

☐ **2005-2006 INTERNAL MEDICINE Q&A REVIEW FOR THE BOARDS**. **> 1300 Q&A** TO PREPARE YOU, © 2005-2006 ☞ $149.00

☐ **2005-2006 AUDIO/VISUAL SLIDE SHOWS for the BOARDS** FEATURING **ALL THE KEY IMAGES YOU'LL NEED TO KNOW IN FULL COLOR, & BEAUTIFULLY PRESENTED IN POWERPOINT**, © 2005-2006 ☞ $495.00

☐ *Why not order a copy as a gift for a student, friend or colleague?* **TURBO MNEMONICS FOR THE BOARDS 2005-2006**: FEATURING >400 MEMORY AIDS TO THE *MOST COMMONLY ASKED* CLINICAL MATERIAL on the BOARDS. © 2005-2006 ☞ $39.95

+ S&H * : $8.00

TOTAL :

3 EASY ORDER OPTIONS:

1. *Fax* orders: 949-203-6178. **FAX THIS FORM**.

2. *E-mail* (or info): FRONTRUNNERS@hotmail.com

3. *Telephone*.: Call Toll-Free: 866-MDBOARDs or 866-IMREVIEW
V/MC/AMEX/Discover/Diners accepted.

SHIPPING ADDRESS:
(Sales tax of 7.75% will be added for all orders shipped within California)
(* Add $8.00 S&H on all orders)

Name: _____

Address: _____

City State Zip: _____

Tel/Fax/Email: _____(emerg only)

(We can ALSO FAX your receipt /confirmation to you within 24h if you request)

PAYMENT OPTIONS: ☐ Money Order ☐ Circle CC: V/MC/AMEX/Discover/Diners

Card number: _____

Name on card: _____Exp. Date _____